SCAMS AND SWINDLERS

SCAMS AND SWINDLERS

An Hachette UK Company
www.hachette.co.uk

Summersdale Publishers
Part of Octopus Publishing Group Limited
Carmelite House
50 Victoria Embankment
LONDON
EC4Y 0DZ
UK

www.summersdale.com

Printed and bound by Clays Ltd, Suffolk, NR35 1ED

ISBN: 978-1-83799-300-0

This FSC® label means that materials used for the product have been responsibly sourced

FSC
www.fsc.org
MIX
Paper | Supporting responsible forestry
FSC® C104740

Substantial discounts on bulk quantities of Summersdale books are available to corporations, professional associations and other organizations. For details contact general enquiries: telephone: +44 (0) 1243 771107 or email: enquiries@summersdale.com.

SCAMS AND SWINDLERS

Shocking True Stories of the
World's Most Daring Con Artists

JAMIE KING

summersdale

All the stories in the book have been at some point expressed in the public domain. Every effort has been made to ensure that all information is correct. Should there be any errors, we apologize and shall be pleased to make the appropriate amendments in any future editions.

DISCLAIMER

Introduction	7
Confidence Trickery	9
Romance Fraud	43
Imposters	65
Forgery	127
Investment Fraud	179
Swindlers	227
Final Word	300

INTRODUCTION

In the 1960s, British rock band The Who sang about not wishing to be fooled again, but when it comes to being scammed and swindled, it happens to us all the time. Why do we fall for the con artists? Whether it's via personal contact or, more likely nowadays, via a text or an email, scammers and swindlers are always finding new ways to ensnare us.

There is a long history of scammers attempting to take money that isn't theirs. Back in the nineteenth century, the term "snake oil salesman" was used to describe those attempting to pass off a product consisting of water and dye as a life-saving potion. They had great success, and this practice still happens today. After a while, even the most cynical person might crack when presented with a must-have offer and hand over their hard-earned cash. You never know, it *might* just work...

The con artist, the scammer, the swindler, the forger, the phisher and the insider trader still operate because they get a return on their schemes. In Britain in 2022, £2,300 was taken by fraudulent means every minute of every day, amounting to £1.2 billion.

For all those who have been caught and appear in these pages, we can only wonder how many escape detection. What scams have been run that we never hear of? Not just those con artists that slipped under the radar and were not spotted, but those that were indeed discovered and, fearing bad publicity, the company or the individuals affected decided not to prosecute?

The schemes we do know about can beggar belief. Among the line-up in our rogue's gallery are: the American man who made thousands from placing farmyard animals' testicles into human males' own scrotums, the fake Czech aristocrat who sold the Eiffel Tower, the Australian woman who made millions by saying alternative therapies saved her from a cancer she didn't have and the Indonesian man who put inferior wine into bottles of famous vintages and sold them at a huge profit. And no book of con artists could miss those giant figures whose names are synonymous with fraud: Charles Ponzi, Frank Abagnale, Bernie Madoff and Han van Meegeren.

The one lesson from this book is to enjoy the tales while also keeping a watchful eye on anyone offering a scheme that might just appear too good to be true. Con artists are skilled in spotting the vulnerable "marks" who they feel sure will fall for their ruses. Don't be one of them!

CONFIDENCE TRICKERY

You might already be familiar with the "Nigerian Prince" scam in which someone claims to be a wealthy individual who needs help to move some funds. They are a constant feature in our email inboxes, but this is just one form of confidence trickery.

Confidence trickery is when the scammer gains the trust of an intended target (known as a "mark") before getting them to hand over money or access to their cash.

Much confidence trickery is done nowadays via electronic communication, whether by telephone, smartphone or laptop. They are used in the same way as older forms of face-to-face or letter correspondence (also known as "mail fraud"). One form of electronically-provided confidence trickery is a crime known in the US as "wire fraud", where a fraudster uses electronic communications to send information to the victim and then receives information or money in return.

We don't know how these scams will look. The stories that follow will show the many different forms that confidence tricks and wire fraud can take. We might just become nostalgic for the Nigerian Prince scam.

YOU'RE FYRED

Music festivals are an established feature in the summer musical event calendar. From giant events like Glastonbury and Coachella to smaller ones that spring up around the world, they promise good music, a chilled atmosphere and, most importantly, a welcome respite from the stresses and strains of the modern world.

The market for festivals is huge, with more and more people willing to shell out for the experience, whether it's for the day or an immersive long weekend. One such festival was the Fyre Festival, due to take place in 2017 on a private island in the Bahamas.

Promoted by models Kendall Jenner, Bella Hadid, Emily Ratajkowski and Hailey Baldwin (or Hailey Bieber, as she is now known), this luxury music festival promised "the best in food, art, music and adventure". The video commercial showed models in both powerboats and swimming in the crystal-clear waters, and DJs played to adoring crowds. Entrepreneur Billy McFarland had rapper Ja Rule alongside as a co-founder of the event, which not only offered sun-kissed fun but also promoted a celebrity booking app which would be produced by McFarland's company, Fyre Media.

McFarland had previously run a credit card membership scheme called Magnises that allowed millennials to sign up for membership so they could attend parties and events. Members paid $250 to receive a black, metal credit card (which worked by using the magnetic strip from their existing cards) and have exclusive access to VIP parties and events such as Johnny Walker whisky tasting or Tesla test drives.

It was not clear how many had signed up. Was it ten thousand? Thirty thousand? A hundred thousand? All these figures were claimed by McFarland. In any case, there had been complaints about tickets for shows that never appeared or refunds never paid.

Social media was key to selling the Fyre Festival. Kendall Jenner was paid $250,000 to make one Instagram post. Within two days, 95 per cent of the six thousand tickets were sold.

Another attractive quality advertised was the location: Norman's Cay, an island organizers claimed was once owned by Colombian drug lord Pablo Escobar. This wasn't true, and when this claim was made in the promotional video, the island's current owners refused permission to hold the event. Great Exuma was then chosen as a replacement. It wasn't a remote private island as advertised, but a much larger one with existing hotels and even an international airport.

Tickets cost between $1,000 and $12,000 and included travel, accommodation, entertainment, food and drink. Attendees would stay in luxury beachside villas with meals prepared by celebrity chefs. Festivalgoers could expect music acts like Blink 182; rappers Skepta, Tyga and Pusha T; synth-pop duo Disclosure; hip hop group Migos; and DJ trio Major Lazer.

Despite the video commercial for Fyre stating, "The actual experience exceeds all expectations", things started to go wrong quickly. Some festivalgoers couldn't even get to the island: their flights from the US were cancelled by the event organizers because there wasn't anywhere for them to stay. The news was broken to the ticket-holders while they were sitting in the airliner.

Those who did make it to the island found that not everything was as advertised. The accommodation was not in beachside villas but disaster-relief tents, and securing one was a free-for-all. Luggage was unceremoniously dropped from the back of a truck. The food, which should have been prepared by celebrity chefs, was, in fact, a cheese slice and some bread, presented in a Styrofoam box. It had rained the night before the first guests arrived, and packaging and mattresses were left lying around the festival site, making it look more like a rubbish dump.

It was immediately apparent that the organizers hadn't been able to coordinate the festival properly. Event organizers say a year is the minimum for such an event. Fyre was being organized and run in two months. It was chaos. One attendee tweeted that it was like *The Hunger Games*. Similarities to *Lord of the Flies* were also expressed.

When $175,000 was needed to cover import fees in order to release four trucks carrying bottled mineral water, currently being held at the airport, McFarland asked his event producer to perform a sex act in lieu of payment. He was going to do it when the customs official relented, as long as he was paid (in money) first.

With events spiralling out of control, music acts pulled out, and the event was cancelled. Attendees queued to get flights back. Some who had just arrived found there were no planes to take them home. They were locked in the island's airport. The islanders who had worked on the festival never received their wages. One business owner paid her staff with her life savings.

The authorities investigated and found that it wasn't just the failed festival that was of interest.

Billy McFarland was arrested and charged with several counts of wire fraud in relation to Fyre Festival and the celebrity booking app. While on bail, McFarland attempted a ticket-selling scam for events such as the Masters, Victoria's Secret shows, the Met Gala and even a chance to meet Taylor Swift.

In 2018, McFarland pleaded guilty to multiple charges, including misleading investors about the financial status of his companies and his own personal wealth. Eighty investors in Fyre Media lost a combined total of $26 million. He was sentenced to six years in prison and ordered to forfeit $26 million.

The judge at McFarland's trial, Naomi Reice Buchwald, called him a "serial fraudster" who had lied throughout his life. Prosecutors described McFarland as "the consummate con artist".

A number of lawsuits ensued, including one for $100 million by 277 Fyre attendees. They eventually got the sum of $281 each. Ja Rule, who avoided any legal implications, sold a Fyre Festival NFT (non-fungible token) for $122,000.

Since his release from federal prison, McFarland has promised a second Fyre Festival and a musical based on the first one.

HOLMES UNDER THE GAVEL

To be a success, a tech start-up company needs a number of crucial elements: a working product, talented employees, adequate funding and good publicity, and it especially helps to have a charismatic face of the company.

Silicon Valley company Theranos had all of these – bar one.

The firm was founded by Elizabeth Holmes. She was born in Washington, D.C. in 1984, the daughter of Christian, a vice president at Enron, and Noel Anne, a congressional staffer. Holmes went to university at Stanford, where she studied chemical engineering.

While at university in 2003, she filed a patent for a wearable patch that would provide medicine to a patient and wirelessly send the results to their doctor, but the idea was unworkable and abandoned. She had also been in Singapore as an intern working on testing for SARS using nasal swabs, and this experience had inspired her to do something different in the field.

In March 2004, Holmes dropped out of university and started working full-time at the company she'd founded, Real-Time Cures. It was going to develop a new approach to blood tests. Holmes soon renamed the company Theranos, from the words "therapy" and "diagnosis".

The technology Theranos was developing was ambitious: it was to disrupt the healthcare technology sector. The device, called an Edison, would be able to test for hundreds of diseases and conditions from just a few drops of blood.

Some of those who Holmes talked to thought it wouldn't work, but one did support the idea: Channing Robertson, who was a professor in chemical engineering at Stanford. Robertson had been her lecturer, and her first class with him was about advanced drug delivery devices, such as patches that released drugs into the body without injection. He became the company's first board member and acted as a technical adviser.

Initial funding came from venture capitalists, who were sold the idea by Holmes. She was the highly-visible face of the company, and she frequently wore black turtlenecks, aping the image of another Silicon Valley entrepreneur, Steve Jobs (although she later claimed it was inspired by Sharon Stone's outfit at the 1996 Oscars). Her red lipstick added to the image that would appear on many magazine covers and newspaper profiles. Holmes also had a distinctive deep baritone voice, which she later admitted was a part of the character she was playing.

By the end of 2004, $6 million had been raised in investments. For its first ten years, the company ran in "stealth" mode. Investments kept coming in, and by 2014, $400 million had been received. Investors included Rupert Murdoch and Oracle founder Larry Ellison. Eventually, $700 million would be put into the company.

The Theranos board contained notable figures such as Henry Kissinger, former secretary of state in President Richard Nixon's government; George Shultz, a former cabinet member of both Nixon and Ronald Reagan; and former US

Marines commander in Afghanistan, General James Mattis. These people lent the company much respectability.

The company emerged from its stealth mode and started a publicity drive. Holmes was featured on the cover of *Fortune* magazine in September 2014. In her profile, Channing Robertson was quoted saying, "I realized that I could have just as well been looking into the eyes of a Steve Jobs or a Bill Gates." By then, Holmes was worth $4.5 billion due to the fact that she held half of Theranos's stock. *Forbes* magazine called her "the youngest self-made female billionaire in the world."

Pharmacy giant Walgreens signed up and started rolling out testing centres. Despite the publicity, Theranos kept secret just how its technology worked. There were no peer-reviewed papers published.

The company soon grew, and by 2015, it had 800 employees. However, a few of them had grave doubts about the product they were working on. One of the main problems was that it didn't work.

Some of the staff decided enough was enough. George Shultz's grandson Tyler worked at Theranos. He became a whistleblower, speaking to journalist John Carreyrou at the *Wall Street Journal*. In October 2015, the newspaper ran a story highlighting doubts surrounding the effectiveness of the Edison, claiming that Theranos was using conventional testing machines instead of their own technology.

Regulators investigated, and the company soon faced civil and criminal legal action. Holmes was arrested. In January 2022, after a 16-week-long trial, she was found guilty on four charges of defrauding investors, three counts of wire fraud and one count of conspiracy to commit wire fraud.

Another senior executive of Theranos also faced charges. Holmes had met Ramesh "Sunny" Balwani when she was 18; he was 37 and had sold a successful tech company he'd founded. They started a relationship which was kept quiet. He joined Theranos in 2009 and became chief operating officer. In a separate trial, Balwani was found guilty of ten counts of wire fraud and two counts of conspiracy to commit wire fraud.

While some lost money and their reputation, there were far more serious effects for others. Ian Gibbons, a British biochemist, was hired as Theranos chief scientist in 2005. He expressed reservations about inaccuracies in the technology's results. When faced with testifying in a civil action, Gibbons had the dilemma of telling the truth and damaging the company and his colleagues or lying and endangering potential customers' health. The night before he was due to give a deposition in May 2013, Gibbons attempted to take his own life. He died in hospital. When Theranos was informed, a company employee asked his widow for the return of Theranos property. His widow was told she'd face legal action if she spoke to the press.

Holmes was given an 11-year sentence, and Balwani received 13 years. They were ordered to repay $452 million.

In May 2023, Holmes went to prison for what the *New York Times* called "one of the most notorious cases of corporate fraud in recent history".

SOMETHING PHISHY

We rely on the internet for our shopping, banking, medical prescriptions, ordering food and drink – pretty much anything and everything. With so much of our lives online, there is always a risk of suffering harm, such as our accounts being hacked and losing personal information or money. This does not only affect individuals – companies both large and small can be affected too.

Phishing is the term used to describe when electronic communications are exploited by scammers to dupe the recipients. It may come in the form of an email that contains a link that, when clicked, will download malware onto a personal computer. This malware can then send data to the scammer, such as credit card details. This attack can also come in the form of ransomware, which will lock off the functions of a website or company's IT services until a payment – or payments – are made.

This is what happened to US company Colonial Pipeline in 2021. Its 5,500 miles of pipeline is a major part of the east of North America's infrastructure, bringing petrol for motor vehicles and aircraft and oil for heating homes from Gulf Coast refineries in Texas right up to New Jersey. Half of the motor vehicle and aircraft fuel for the East Coast comes via the pipeline – at a rate of 100 million gallons a day.

On 6 May 2021, hackers managed to get into Colonial's IT network via a single-factor VPN (virtual private network) password. (More secure systems use two-factor authentication.) The hackers downloaded 100 gigabytes of data within a two-hour time period. They then left ransomware in the system, locking out computers and affecting the billing and accounting areas of the company.

The cybercriminals left a ransom note in Colonial's network, letting them know they had breached the company's IT infrastructure. The cyberattackers threatened to leak the stolen data unless the ransom money was paid. They wanted 75 bitcoins (or $4.4 million). The ransom was paid by Colonial the day after the attack to get its systems up and running, restart the oil supply and have its stolen data returned. They also called in a cybersecurity company to investigate the incident.

The hackers had used DarkSide, a type of Ransomware-as-a-Service (RaaS). It is available on the dark web, and its developers make money whenever a cybercrime group use it.

Colonial had shut down the pipeline to prevent any risk of the malware affecting it. It was reported that this was done because the organization would be unable to bill customers using their fuel after the attack. The shutdown caused alarm since, with the supply halted, vehicle drivers rushed to panic-buy fuel. Long queues formed at gas stations in several states, including Alabama, Georgia and Florida. Price gouging took place as garage operators took the opportunity to increase prices. Some drivers filled plastic bags with petrol, leading to a warning from the US Consumer Product Safety Commission that asked people not to store the flammable liquid this way. Airlines were also affected, and American Airlines ran out of jet fuel.

The US president, Joe Biden, urged calm and asked vehicle drivers to only buy what fuel they needed. He issued emergency orders allowing more fuel from other suppliers to be delivered.

It took days for the supply to be restored. The pipeline only started up again on 12 May since the decryption key supplied by the hackers took several days to work. Even with this key, Colonial's finance systems were still being brought back to operation a month later.

In June, the US Department of Justice's Ransomware and Digital Extortion Task Force announced they had recovered 63.7 bitcoins ($2.3 million as the price of the cryptocurrency had since fallen) of the ransom paid. Who the hackers were has not been discovered. President Biden stated that US intelligence agencies suspected that they were located in Russia but were not acting on the orders of the Russian government.

TERRORS FROM THE DEEPFAKE

For a parent, the kidnapping of their child is a terrifying prospect. When that kidnapping is proven to be not real but, in fact, the result of an Artificial Intelligence (AI) deepfake, it adds another layer to the fear and anxiety.

In January 2023, Jennifer DeStefano, a mother of two children, answered her phone. She had just collected her youngest daughter from a dance class in Scottsdale, Arizona; her 15-year-old daughter Brie was away skiing with her father. DeStefano didn't recognize the number displayed on her screen but, as her daughter was away, thought she should answer it, just in case. She heard her daughter crying and saying, "Mom, these bad men have me, help me, help me."

A man then said she would be freed in return for $1 million. If DeStefano alerted the authorities, he would rape her daughter and leave her in Mexico; DeStefano would never see her daughter again. While she tried to contact Brie or Brie's father, DeStefano was able to negotiate, managing to lower the ransom demand to $50,000.

Before any money was exchanged, the terrified mother managed to contact her daughter to find out she was completely unaware of any potential harm. DeStefano had been fooled; Brie's voice had been cloned using AI technology. A small snippet of a voice on social media can be sampled and used to say anything. Other samples of screaming or crying from TV or movies are added into the audio mix.

Vishing (voice phishing) is part of what is known as "social engineering", where personal information is gathered and used by the scammer against an individual or a business. In 2023, hotel and entertainment company MGM Resorts experienced a ransomware attack thought to have originated from a vishing phone call. The details of an employee were taken from LinkedIn, and then the scammer phoned the MGM IT help desk, where they got log-in credentials. Once in the company's IT network, they launched the malware. The MGM's Las Vegas Strip casinos saw their slot machines, hotel elevators and electronic door keys stop working. After a similar cyberattack, Caesars Entertainment – owners of famous Las Vegas hotel Caesars Palace – paid a ransom amount of $15 million to have their systems restored.

The vishing scam is not limited to the US. In Saskatchewan, Canada, two grandparents were contacted by their grandson, Brandon. He said he was in jail with no money and needed cash to get bail. They withdrew three thousand Canadian dollars from one bank and then went to another. When there, the bank manager told them that they had seen similar actions before and that it was probably a scam. The couple realized they had been duped.

While those in these examples didn't pay any money to the scammers, others have not been so fortunate. The parents of Canadian Benjamin Perkin were phoned by a lawyer. He told them Benjamin had been involved in a car accident in which he'd killed a US diplomat and needed money to pay legal fees.

This lawyer put Benjamin on the phone. His parents were unsure but convinced enough by his voice to send Canadian $21,000 via Bitcoin. It was only through speaking to Benjamin later that day that they realized they had been scammed.

In a congressional hearing following her deepfake experience, DeStefano said, "There is no limit to the depth of evil AI can enable."

SMISH HITS

Smishing is another form of electronic fraud. As the name suggests, it is an amalgam of SMS (texting) and phishing. Smishing is very similar to phishing by email: an authentic-looking message sent by the scammer contains a link. The link will take the recipient to a malicious website asking to input their confidential information, or it could install malware on the recipient's phone, sometimes in the form of an app. Once installed, it will send private information, such as credit card details, to the scammer.

Computer users are more aware of phishing attempts via email, but there is more trust for messages received on mobile phones. They appear more personal. Phone users also believe their phones are less likely to be infiltrated with malware than computers, and two-thirds of them don't realize when they are on the receiving end of smishing attacks. This lowering of scepticism allows the scammer a greater chance of succeeding.

To detect email phishing on a computer, you can use the mouse to hover over the link, which will display the destination URL at the bottom of the browser, allowing you to establish whether it is a legitimate website or not – something that is not possible with a mobile device. The scammer can also hide the true mobile number with a decoy, which may be a legitimate organization's number, in a method called "spoofing".

The volume of smishing attempts is growing. In April 2022, an average of 2.7 billion smishing texts were sent. There are many different formats for smishing texts. Some examples include:

- A bank or credit card provider asks the recipient to send their account information as there has been unusual activity on their account or the account has been locked for some reason.
- A gift opportunity. This will offer the phone user the chance to claim a free gift, reward points or a money-off offer. A smishing attempt in 2020 offered a free iPhone for respondents who gave their credit card details to pay for a shipping fee.
- An order confirmation. An invoice will be sent from a retailer asking for confirmation of the order or from a parcel delivery company asking for confirmation of the item being delivered. A scam in 2020 saw users receive messages supposedly from FedEx. It asked the recipient to confirm delivery preferences for a package. The link in the message was to a fake Amazon page where taking part in a customer satisfaction survey would result in receiving a free gift – after handing over credit card details.

There are even smishing scams involving healthcare. While it may seem deplorable to take advantage of fears during a pandemic, this is exactly what some scammers did. In the US in 2020, messages were sent directing people to an online Covid-19 test. Luckily, most recipients realized that this wasn't possible. In Australia, fraudsters offered recipients guidelines on how to get tested. The links in these messages were not to a government website but to one that downloaded malware.

Not all the smishing scammers are caught. One that was, however, was involved in a healthcare scam.

In May 2021, at the Old Bailey in London, 21-year-old Teige Gallagher was sentenced to jail for four years and three months for committing fraud by false representation and for being in possession of articles for use in fraud. Gallagher was tracked down by the Dedicated Card and Payment Crime Unit, a joint unit of London's Metropolitan and City police forces.

Posing as someone working for the NHS (National Health Service), the Londoner had sent text messages offering Covid vaccinations. He set up fake web pages that mimicked the UK government site's layout. To verify their identity and secure vaccinations, those duped would have to give personal details, including addresses, bank account details and credit card details.

Gallagher used several smartphones to send messages purporting to be from banks, mobile phone networks, Her Majesty's Revenue and Customs, and streaming service Netflix. On one phone, he had 2,000 numbers. A SIM farm (devices that hold several SIM cards and facilitate bulk sending of scam texts) was also found in his home.

It is not just individuals at risk of these scams. Employers are also being targeted. In 2022, with increased remote working and company-issued smartphones, three-quarters of companies in the US received smishing messages.

MILLER TIME

Social media influencers play a part in many of our lives. Their beautifully composed and carefully chosen images of them living their best lives are a feature of our insatiable curiosity about how others spend their time. One influencer, however, was not just getting likes and comments; she was getting government money.

The Covid-19 pandemic impacted all aspects of everyone's lives. Besides the health effects on countless millions, economies faced severe problems as companies saw massive reductions in income. Governments took action by shoring up the income of individuals through furlough schemes and loans.

Danielle Miller grew up in Manhattan, the daughter of wealthy parents, and was educated at the prestigious private Horace Mann School. Her father, a lawyer, was a former New York State Bar Association president.

In the eighth grade, Miller got into trouble when she sent sexually explicit videos to a male classmate as part of a dare. The videos were circulated, and the 13-year-old was humiliated. Miller admitted later that she became a different person, growing into an active partygoer. After leaving high school, Miller enrolled at Arizona State University, but her notoriety followed her there.

After graduating, Miller moved to Los Angeles and enjoyed the nightlife while working in PR. She was friends with Paris Hilton's brother Barron and started going out with a well-known DJ. While in Los Angeles, she reconnected with someone she knew from her high school days. The friend hung out with her until she discovered that five bank cheques had been paid to Miller from her account, something that Miller denied ever happening.

In 2016, she started studying at law school outside Los Angeles, and after her first year, interned for a New York judge during the summer break. Miller would often visit a spa on the Upper West Side, running up a $5,000 bill she paid with stolen credit card details. She was arrested and charged with identity theft and grand larceny.

When Miller was released, she returned to California. There, she met Mackinzie Dae, an ex-US marine working in marketing. They set up a PR company together, but after the relationship ended, he accused her of setting up credit cards and loans in his name.

Miller missed a court appearance in connection with the credit card theft because she had gone to Mexico to celebrate her birthday. She was arrested as she returned to the US and sent to Rikers Island prison for a year. When Miller entered Rikers, she received tips on how to survive imprisonment from an inmate called Anna Sorokin, also known as Anna Delvey, "the Fake Heiress" of Netflix fame. While there, Miller also met another scammer, Ciera Blas. In 2015, Blas had been arrested for credit card fraud, the money being used to fund a shopping spree. Blas used her Instagram account to show off the goods she had obtained. She was apprehended in the Manhattan luxury department store Bergdorf Goodman.

Miller was released from Rikers in the summer of 2019 with only $30 and a travel card to her name. Her parents had disassociated themselves from her, and she had to use associates from Rikers for help. In early 2020, Miller bumped into Blas, who had been released shortly after her. Blas recruited her as a "trapper" – someone who was able to act as the person whose identity had been stolen.

Miller and Blas spent the first Covid lockdown in spring 2020 in Miami, Florida. When the lockdown ended, the pair went shopping, with Miller impersonating a woman from Los Angeles whose details had been stolen in a burglary. They drove around in Porsche sports cars and Jaguars. The two then tried to withdraw $8,000 using the same identity at a drive-through bank. Bank employees were suspicious and called the police. When Miller and Blas were arrested, they were found in possession of fake driver's licences using Miller's photograph, as well as credit cards and $25,000 in cash. Blas bailed out Miller, who relied on another Rikers alum to give her a roof over her head.

With the pandemic still very much prevalent, the US government offered loans to those struggling financially. Starting in July 2020, Miller made at least ten applications to receive money, including Economic Injury Disaster Loan funds through the Small Business Administration as well as Pandemic Unemployment Assistance. She used fake identities for individuals and companies. Funds totalling $1.5 million were received. The money was used to rent a luxury apartment and to buy clothes from Chanel, Gucci and Prada and other luxury goods like watches from Rolex and handbags from Louis Vuitton.

Miller's 30,000-plus followers on Instagram saw her with her ill-gotten gains. She posted videos on TikTok of her driving a Rolls-Royce convertible with a Louis Vuitton bag on her lap. This wasn't the end of her spending: she flew on private jets to California from Florida to stay at a luxury hotel. For this trip, she used the same stolen ID to book the jet and the hotel.

Money was also spent on something more personal: a Brazilian butt lift. In May 2021, while recovering from the surgery, Miller was arrested by federal agents. They found fake IDs, fake bank cards, tens of thousands of dollars in cash and a smartphone with messages from Miller in the guise of someone else.

In March 2023, Miller pleaded guilty to three counts of wire fraud and two counts of aggravated identity theft. Each wire fraud charge could have earned her a 20-year prison sentence and a quarter-million-dollar fine. Aggravated identity fraud came with a two-year sentence. In June 2023, Miller received a jail sentence of six years, to overlap the previous five-year sentence she'd received for bank fraud in Florida.

Miller was also ordered to hand over $1.3 million. While on house arrest awaiting trial in the autumn of 2022, Miller said in an interview, "I more so consider myself a con artist than anything." As of August 2023, she still has over 30,000 Instagram followers.

SCAMDEMIC

Miller wasn't the only one to take public money intended for those truly suffering financial hardship during the pandemic. In the UK, £47 billion was issued in the government-backed Bounce Back Loan scheme launched in May 2020. It was the biggest of the three UK Covid-related government loan schemes to protect businesses from going under, the other two being business interruption loan schemes.

Small and micro-sized businesses could borrow a sum from £2,000 up to 25 per cent of turnover, with a maximum amount of £50,000, to be used for business purposes and not for personal purchases. A low interest rate of 2.5 per cent was applied to the loan, available from 24 accredited lenders such as banks and building societies.

Those applying didn't have to sign a personal guarantee. The UK government acted as the loan guarantor, meaning that if the borrowers didn't repay, the UK taxpayer would have to cover the cost. Applicants for these "bounce back" loans applied online, and checks on the veracity of those claiming were not too thorough.

A quarter of UK businesses were recipients of the loans: 1.6 million companies received money. They had to pay the money back over a six or ten-year period. Most loans went to very small businesses with a turnover of under £632,000.

The scheme was open to opportunistic fraudsters. The UK's counter-fraud minister, Lord Agnew, resigned in 2022, citing the government's poor and "desperately inadequate" measures to halt any fraud or abuse of the funds. As the emphasis was on processing the loans quickly, there was not much in the way of scrutiny. In 2022, the government stated it would lose £17 billion from the scheme, with £1.1 billion lost via fraud.

Fraudulent claims included one by the owner of a car breakdown recovery business in Newport, Wales, who claimed a £50,000 loan. Half of the money was used to buy a new tow truck, with the other half spent on drugs. He then sold the new vehicle to buy more drugs.

There was also a self-employed roofer from Tamworth who asked a third party to make the application for a loan. The roofer received £13,000, far more than he was entitled to, which he gambled away in just three weeks.

A director who gave his company's address as an Indian restaurant in Wrexham claimed £50,000. The company was liquidated in 2022 with debts totalling over £150,000. Insolvency investigators discovered that the company had ceased trading in 2019 and that the restaurant was owned by a different company. Similarly, a husband and wife running a Mexican chicken takeaway claimed the full loan of £50,000 by saying their company's turnover was £200,000 when it was nearer to £40,000. When they came under investigation, they paid back the money, but it was not enough to prevent both receiving jail sentences.

Then there was the businessman in London who received £25,000 and then shut down his consultancy business so that he wouldn't have to pay back the money. He transferred the loan money to his personal bank accounts. He was given a six-month suspended prison sentence.

Some people even claimed money by setting up companies that never traded. A total of £500,000 was claimed by a group of 11 companies registered in four locations across the UK: Berkshire, Lancashire, London and Shropshire. The Insolvency Service found no evidence of trading premises for the companies or that they had ever traded. Nine of the companies went for the maximum of £50,000, with one claiming two loans' worth of £100,000. The money raised was eventually transferred to Hong Kong.

But perhaps the most surprising and shocking use of these funds was by a London barbershop owner who sent over £10,000 of his Bounce Back loan to fund the Islamic State terrorist group in Syria. He was given a 12-year jail sentence.

And finally, the biggest Bounce Back loan fraud was orchestrated by a Russian and a Lithuanian man who were both jailed in March 2023 for a total of 33 years for laundering £70 million of money from criminal gangs. Ten million of this originated from Bounce Back loans. The two of them were out on bail when the pandemic began and were able to borrow large amounts. One of the UK banks gave them £3.2 million. The money was distributed through shell companies.

These are only some of the cases that are known about and where punishments have been issued to the guilty parties. Those running companies caught defrauding the country's finances could also face being banned from running companies at all. Over 750 company directors were disqualified after abusing the support schemes.

ONECOIN TO CON THE WORLD

There is an old expression in politics, often attributed to US President Abraham Lincoln, that you can fool some of the people all of the time, you can fool all of the people some of the time, but you can't fool all of the people all of the time. Ruja Ignatova and Sebastian Greenwood certainly fooled many of the people for long enough to sell their cryptocurrency.

Cryptocurrencies are digital currencies not issued by central banks. They are encrypted, impossible to forge and come with their own virtual ledger, known as a blockchain. The blockchain is impossible to be tampered with. The first cryptocurrency was Bitcoin, launched in 2009. Early investors made fortunes after huge interest in acquiring this new form of currency. Other cryptocurrencies followed, eager to cash in on the popular innovation. One of these was OneCoin, the product of OneCoin Limited, co-founded in 2014 by Ignatova and Greenwood.

Ignatova was born in Bulgaria in 1980 and was ten when her family emigrated to Germany. She gained her doctorate from a German university in 2005 and a master's in Law at Oxford University in the UK before working at consultancy company McKinsey for six years.

Ignatova was the glamorous face of cryptocurrency: often dressed in ball gowns, with diamond jewellery and her trademark red lipstick. Ignatova called herself the "Cryptoqueen", and Greenwood used the letters "HRH" on his contacts list: Her Royal Highness.

Greenwood was born in Sweden and graduated with a degree in marketing and finance from the private Regent's University in London. He worked in PR and then network marketing. On his LinkedIn page, Greenwood stated he had been involved in five unsuccessful ventures. One of these was a social media channel called SiteTalk, to be the "next Facebook". He had learned a lesson as these failures taught him "how to be more selective when choosing a potential business endeavour".

The two met in 2013 at a cryptocurrency seminar in Singapore. The next year, they rolled out OneCoin. Based in Sofia, Bulgaria, this new cryptocurrency was marketed and sold via a global multi-level marketing (MLM) network of members. These members obtained commission when they recruited others to buy cryptocurrency trader packages in the style of a classic pyramid scheme. Prices started at €100 and went all the way up to €118,000. Investors were promised a fivefold or even a tenfold return on their money.

Ignatova spoke at large public events, such as Coin Rush at London's vast Wembley Arena in June 2016 in front of 3,000 fans. She was the centrepiece of these live events, extolling the virtues of the project, which would become the number one cryptocurrency in the world. Some observers described these live events as verging on the cult-like.

Some investors were convinced of the authenticity of the scheme by a video of Ignatova speaking at a conference on economic development organized by the prestigious

Economist magazine. The video claimed she was asked to speak at the event. But she was actually only on stage because OneCoin had partially sponsored the event.

Another factor in the supposed legitimacy was Ignatova's appearance on the cover of *Fortune* magazine in 2015. The cover was reproduced and widely distributed, but it was not what it seemed. Ignatova had indeed appeared in the magazine, but only in the Bulgarian edition and only in an advert she had paid for, designed to look exactly like the magazine's front cover.

The strategy worked. Over $4 billion was invested by at least 3.5 million people between 2014 and 2016.

The marketing told those interested in purchasing OneCoin that it was going to kill off Bitcoin with its "unique and innovative cryptocurrency". The investors faced one major problem: OneCoin wasn't a proper cryptocurrency. To convince them that OneCoin was legitimate, investors were told that tokens included in their trader packages could be used to gain positions in "mining pools", in other words, computer hardware that "mined" (produced) OneCoin. Neither the mining pools nor computers existed. In 2015, the two founders had emailed each other to discuss the issue of them selling "fake coins", those that didn't exist in OneCoin's blockchain, the ledger where all transactions are meant to be stored. When Ignatova emailed Greenwood on this subject, she used the phrase "We are f**ed".

Ignatova and Greenwood misled buyers – or "idiots", as Greenwood referred to them once – by stating that the price of the coins was subject to the market forces of supply and demand. In reality, the price was set by them. Each coin's value went up from €0.50 to €29.95 by January 2019.

The price never fell because they weren't being traded on an open public exchange like other cryptocurrencies.

As the mastermind behind the use of an MLM (multi-level marketing) structure to promote OneCoin, Greenwood earned 5 per cent of sales, earning him an estimated $300 million. He enjoyed the high life on other people's money, spending it on stays at a five-star resort in Brazil, a luxury beach-view villa in Koh Samui in Thailand and a five-star hotel in Barcelona in Spain. He was also able to buy properties in Dubai, Spain and Thailand. There was plenty of money left over for designer clothes and watches and a deposit on a half-million-pound yacht. To travel between his acquired real estate, Greenwood had the use of a private jet.

Ignatova's money bought her a luxury penthouse in London, a Dubai penthouse, two properties in Bulgaria, jewellery, and paintings by the likes of Andy Warhol. For her birthday party, held at London's Victoria and Albert Museum, she hired legendary singer Tom Jones.

In 2016, speculation grew on the internet that OneCoin was a fraud. Members couldn't sell their coins, and their ability to withdraw real currency was limited. Some had warned about Ignatova but weren't listened to. The British Financial Conduct Authority posted a warning notice on its website, but coming under pressure from OneCoin's lawyers, it took the notice down.

There was a sign that those in charge of the scheme were not spotlessly clean. In 2016, Ignatova pleaded guilty to fraud and other charges in Germany following the bankruptcy of a metal factory she'd acquired in 2009. She was given a suspended prison sentence and fined €18,000.

Investigations by the authorities resulted in the Cryptoqueen being charged with fraud and money laundering in the US District Court in New York on 12 October 2017. A federal warrant was issued for her arrest. Two weeks later, on 25 October, Ignatova flew from Sofia to Athens on a commercial flight. Despite her wealth, she flew on budget airline Ryanair. This was the last time she was seen publicly. Her brother, who pleaded guilty to fraud and money laundering charges, said she took $500 million with her.

In June 2022, the FBI put Ignatova on their "Ten Most Wanted" list of fugitives, with an expanded list of charges: wire fraud, conspiracy to commit wire fraud, conspiracy to commit money laundering, conspiracy to commit securities fraud and securities fraud charges. A reward of $250,000 is offered to anyone with information that would lead to her arrest. Those who may come in contact with her are warned she is believed to travel with armed guards. Identifying this once highly visible figure may be made harder as she might have had cosmetic procedures. Rumours have abounded: is she on maternity leave? In Russia? Living in Dubai? On a yacht in the Black Sea? Or has she been killed by Albanian gangsters?

Greenwood was arrested in Thailand in July 2018 and extradited to the US to face fraud and money laundering charges. In September 2023, he was given a 20-year jail sentence for his part in the fraudulent scheme and ordered to forfeit $300 million.

US attorney Damian Williams said OneCoin was "one of the largest fraud schemes ever perpetrated".

NIGERIAN PRINCE

The Nigerian Prince scam seems to have been around for as long as the internet. Emails arrive telling of how a prince or another high-ranking member of society has run into trouble. They have vast amounts of money but are unable to access it at this particular time. They promise that if the recipient were to take action to help, they would be very well rewarded. All the recipient has to do is either forward money to help the troubled VIP through this difficult time or provide their bank details so that the prince can transfer a large amount of money due to them for helping in this traumatic time. Reasons given are almost limitless but can include kidnapped children, bank accounts frozen, an inheritance paid into a foreign bank, a payment due for being scammed, or a Nigerian astronaut being stranded in space.

The Nigerian Prince is a phishing attempt, also known as an advance fee fraud or a 419 fraud, due to that number being taken from the Nigerian Criminal Code for such scams, which states that "Any person who by any false pretence, and with intent to defraud, obtains from any other person anything capable of being stolen, or induces any other person to deliver to any person anything capable of being stolen, is guilty of a felony, and is liable to imprisonment for three years."

The scam gained an association with that African country due to the prevalence of scam schemes there. A range of reasons have been provided as to why Nigeria in particular. It is thought that in the 1990s, high unemployment and the lack of a welfare state provision in the country – coupled with the advent of internet cafés – allowed the untraceable sending of such scam emails. For a motive, many Nigerians believed corruption in the higher ranks of society contributed to a wealth gap between rich and poor. Without good-paying jobs, pursuing internet-based income was one way of getting money. There is also a train of thought that colonialism has hugely impacted the country, and this was one way of receiving some sort of reparation. While the same type of scam was attempted in other countries, the negative associations with Nigeria have stuck to the present day. Nigerian-originating financial instruments such as cheques are viewed with suspicion and even emails from the country are blocked by internet service providers across the world.

Although it is thought of as an internet-based scam, the concept goes back much further. For example, the "Spanish Prisoner" swindle originates from the eighteenth century. Someone acting for a person imprisoned in Spain asked for money to bribe the guards or pay bail money. Once the prisoner was out, it was promised that further money would be forthcoming to the victim.

The fact that the clichéd Nigerian Prince emails are still sent out does not mean a lack of thought by the scammers. It is deliberate because it assumes that those not likely to fall for the content of the emails will immediately delete them or consign them to their spam folder. There are key parts of these phishing emails that will put off the aware recipient: they contain many spelling or grammatical errors, the amounts of money being mentioned are huge, and the messages are not personally addressed. Those who don't immediately delete are those who might be tempted. If they have fallen for the far-fetched story at the start, then there is a greater chance they will send the money.

Some certainly are still falling for this scam. In 2019, $700,000 was lost in the US to the Nigerian Prince scam. With a long history and continued success, it seems our inboxes will continue to be filled with missives about down-on-their-luck foreign royalty.

ROMANCE FRAUD

It is said that money can't buy love, but when it comes to romance fraud, there is a lot of money at stake. In 2022, romance scams in the US accounted for $740 million in losses from 19,000 victims.

A romance scam is when someone looking for love is targeted by a fraudster. The lovelorn will be charmed and perhaps even wined and dined until the target begins to fall in love. When the bond of trust has been established, the fraudster will begin the con – obtaining money from the victim on a one-off occasion or through a long con until they are rumbled or the victim's money runs out.

The heartless scammer will have no compulsion about preying on the unsuspecting who are only looking for some companionship. If they sense the target will produce financial rewards, they will keep the con going; if the intended victim seems reluctant or is too suspicious, they will just move on to the next person they can "woo".

While the Everly Brothers sang that love hurts, it can also destroy a person's bank balance. The romance fraud victim is not only left with a broken heart but also broken finances.

DIAMONDS NOT FOREVER

Finding that perfect soul mate is not always easy. In the past, those looking for love had to go to pubs and clubs or wait until that right moment at the office Christmas party. With the advent of technology, things got much easier. Sign up to an online dating site and it is just a case of swiping right – or left – to find that significant other.

In 2017, Norwegian woman Cecilie Fjellhøy was on dating app Tinder when she came across the profile of Simon Leviev. He was a billionaire's son, his father Lev Leviev having made his fortune from the diamond industry, and Simon had followed into the business. His Instagram showed him on yachts, private jets, and staying in expensive hotels. What was not to like?

Cecilie swiped right. Simon was in London, as was she, so they met up. He was romantic, sending her messages and huge bouquets of roses. Cecilie was literally swept off her feet when he took her to Europe on a private jet.

Then things changed. Simon told her he was in danger and sent photos of his bodyguard, Peter, bloodied in an ambulance. They had been attacked and weren't safe. Simon told her that those pursuing him were able to track his movements through his credit card and asked if she could give him her American Express card to use. This she did.

He asked for money, and she took out a loan to cover the $25,000 in cash he wanted taken to Amsterdam for him. As soon as he had the money, Simon said he had to leave and flew to Stockholm. Once in Stockholm, Simon met up with Pernilla Sjoholm, another woman he had met via Tinder. As friends, they enjoyed a tour around Europe – with Simon's new girlfriend, Polina.

More and more requests for money came in until Cecilie had racked up debts of $250,000 with nine different creditors. When she went to American Express, they told her that Simon was not who he said he was. Investigations by a Norwegian newspaper discovered he was actually born Shimon Hayut, an Israeli man with an upbringing in the ultra-Orthodox city of Bnei Brak. He had a previous conviction in Finland, where he had spent two years in jail for defrauding three women before being deported back to Israel. He was not the son of a billionaire.

Simon had begun his life of crime after leaving the Navy as part of his Israeli national service. He forged a cheque and bought a car with the proceeds. Then, in 2010, aged 19, he left the country on a forged passport.

In 2019, when another girlfriend, Ayleen Charlotte, found out about her boyfriend's true nature – having given him $140,000 – she exacted revenge by selling off his clothes and keeping the money. When she found out which flight he was on, she alerted the police. Simon was arrested in Athens and later sentenced to 15 months in jail in Israel for using a fake passport. He served five months.

Was Simon running a Ponzi scheme? Using the money from one victim to fund a lifestyle being enjoyed by him and another woman? Media reports claimed he was given $10 million from women he knew. He is now banned from using Tinder but has talked about setting up his own dating app. For income, he sells personalized video birthday greetings. In 2023, plans were revealed for a reality TV programme called *The Simon Show*.

Some of the women he scammed have talked openly about their experiences, hoping their testimonies will help those looking for love in the future to be more wary of someone who seems perfect. In 2022, Ayleen Charlotte, Cecilie Fjellhøy and Pernilla Sjoholm set up a crowdfunding appeal to help pay off the debts they had accumulated. They raised over £180,000.

In an interview with an Israeli newspaper in 2023, Simon said about Cecilie's appearance in a Netflix documentary called *The Tinder Swindler*, "The fact that a person cries in an interview doesn't mean it actually happened."

THE SPY WHO CONNED ME

People wishing to impress might hint at having a more exciting or interesting job. Telling an intended romantic partner that they are a pilot might have more of an impact than admitting to being a shelf stacker at the local supermarket.

One man who made himself out to be something extraordinary was Robert Freegard. He worked in a bar and then in car dealerships as a salesman. It was through these occupations that he met some of the people whose lives he would hugely impact.

In 1993, he convinced three students at an agricultural college in England that he was an agent for MI5 – Britain's internal security service – and that they were in danger from an IRA terrorist cell. Freegard told them a student who had committed suicide had actually been shot by the terrorists. They now had to flee because his cover had been blown.

The group went on the road and were told by Freegard not to tell anyone where they were. He moved them from place to place, getting them to have menial jobs to pay for his protection. Months on the run became years.

Freegard insisted the students ask for money from their parents. One of the students, John Atkinson, convinced his parents to provide over £400,000 and another – Sarah

Smith – a £200,000 inheritance. Maria Hendy, who had been Freegard's girlfriend when they fled, had two children by him and eventually spent nine years with him. He adopted her surname to become "Robert Hendy-Freegard" in an attempt to procure money from her parents. They were not fooled and did not hand over any cash.

Hendy-Freegard had a modus operandi he used several times. He would charm his victims into believing his lies, distance them from friends and family and exert greater and greater control over them. At times, he would threaten violence or be violent. He beat up John Atkinson to toughen him up and assaulted his wife Maria repeatedly, resulting in her losing teeth and suffering broken ankles.

He was also well-versed in humiliating his targets. One, a white woman, was asked to walk through London streets while dressed in an Indian wedding outfit. He convinced one man called Simon Young to travel from Sheffield to Manchester to buy a can opener from a specific shop, then hand it to a named person in a London pub as part of his training to be an agent. He had to buy a copy of *Gay Times* and read it on the train. Young found out it was a ruse when Hendy-Freegard openly laughed at him for doing it.

Hendy-Freegard spent time with other women, one being an American psychologist called Kim Adams, who had met him through buying a car. Her stepfather had won the lottery in Arizona. Rob would phone attempting to get money, the supposed justification being that Kim wanted to become a spy and there were training fees due. In May 2003, the police and FBI arranged that Kim's mother would hand over £10,000 in person at Heathrow airport. The bait worked – Robert was arrested, and Kim released from his grasp.

Following the arrest, evidence emerged of other women who had fallen under Hendy-Freegard's spell. Company director Renata Kister was persuaded to buy a new car at the Sheffield garage where he worked. Hendy-Freegard then kept the profit from the sale of her old car. She also took out a £15,000 loan for him.

Civil servant Leslie Gardner lost £16,000 through him needing money for a range of reasons, including to pay off the IRA, buy himself out of the police force and provide for his sick mother.

Hendy-Freegard had an affair with newly married Elizabeth Bartholomew and then threatened to show her husband explicit photographs. She took out £14,500 in loans for him and, as part of a "test", was told to sleep rough, spending weeks on park benches.

Lawyer Caroline Cowper had £14,000 taken from her building society account, as well as losing £8,000 of the money for her car's sale he had overseen. He bought a £7,000 engagement ring for her with money he'd taken from her bank account.

In 2004, Hendy-Freegard was put on trial for charges of kidnapping, theft and deception. Found guilty, he was sentenced to life imprisonment, though his appeal resulted in him being found not guilty of kidnapping, and he was released in 2009. This wasn't the end of his story. In the autumn of 2022, Hendy-Freegard was extradited to France on charges of attempted murder.

PEACHES AND CREAMING OFF THE MONEY

Romance fraud is a particularly insensitive and cruel crime. Preying on those looking for a partner and playing on their emotions requires a certain type of swindler. When the target is an octogenarian survivor of the Holocaust, there are few words left to describe the perpetrator once "despicable", "evil" and "lowest of the low" have been used.

One such criminal is Peaches Stergo, a 36-year-old woman from Florida.

In May 2017, she met her future victim on a dating website. Stergo then told the man, who was looking for companionship, that she needed money to pay her lawyer in order to release a settlement due to her for injuries received in a car accident. The victim sent the first cheque for $25,000. It would be the first of over sixty.

Stergo continued to ask for money for the next four and a half years. She said she would pay the victim back and needed extra money to gain access to a bank account to do so.

There was no lawyer, no legal settlement and no intention of paying the money back. The heartless scammer faked a bank employee's email address to provide authentication that the money had been paid into the bank. She also faked invoices to assure the victim's bank that the money was being legitimately paid.

Stergo enjoyed the money, spending it on a $300,000 gated community home in Florida, a condo, two $60,000 cars, a boat, vacations in luxury hotels and designer clothes.

Stergo had a partner, and she texted them to admit to not wanting to earn money through legitimate employment, saying, "I don't want to work... it's too hard." She also laughed at her victim for saying he loved her.

She conned her victim out of $2.8 million, taking all his life savings. When the victim told his son in October 2021 that his savings had gone, his son worked out straight away his father had been defrauded.

The police were contacted, and Stergo was arrested. She pleaded guilty to wire fraud and was sentenced to four years and three months in prison. She was also ordered to pay $2.8 million in restitution and forfeit the property and luxury goods she had bought with the victim's money. The judge called her "unbelievably cruel", a person who was motivated by greed.

The 87-year-old victim, who'd emigrated to the US following his parents' death in the Holocaust, had gone on to build a successful business in New York before retiring. He told the judge, "The last thing I expected was to finish my days in the same manner that I started them — penniless and betrayed."

PEOPLE ARE STRANGIS

A compelling person who convinces victims of their circumstances – no matter how unbelievable – and who is able to acquire money from them while putting them through emotional and physical turmoil is a common theme among romance fraudsters. In the UK, Robert Hendy-Freegard was one, and on the other side of the Atlantic, Anthony Strangis was another.

In 2011, Strangis met Sarma Melngailis online.

Melngailis was the owner of a successful restaurant in Manhattan called Pure Food and Wine. It was a pioneer in the vegan raw food movement, where nothing was cooked. The fine dining restaurant, which opened in 2004, welcomed celebrity diners such as supermodel Gisele Bündchen, former president Bill Clinton and film star Alec Baldwin – who met his future wife Hilaria there. In 2005, Melngailis opened a takeaway next door to the restaurant called One Lucky Duck. She had a tattoo inked of the duck logo on her upper left arm.

She encountered Strangis when he was replying to Alec Baldwin on Twitter. Melngailis had tried to persuade the actor to buy a dog but had instead bought one herself, a pit bull she named Leon. When they met in person at the end of 2011, Strangis was mysterious about his occupation, alluding to being involved in some sort of secret government Black Ops operation.

When Melngailis had first met Strangis, he'd gone under the name "Shane Fox". When she discovered this, he explained it away by saying he needed extra identities for his covert activities.

Strangis claimed to have money. They looked at $15 million townhouses, and he took her to Tiffany's and said she could have anything she wanted. He took her to a private banker, but the funds he'd promised never materialized. Melngailis was in debt for a couple of million dollars after the purchase of her restaurant, and he told her he'd be able to clear that.

Melngailis wasn't initially sure about the relationship, but Strangis told her he'd been looking for her all his life, and it was fate that had brought them together. After a year together, they got married in 2012. Strangis omitted to tell his new bride that he had been married before. In 2004, he'd met a Florida woman called Stacy Avery, and they married after going out for three months. He told Stacy he had been left $5 million by an aunt – money that never transpired. Despite having a child with Stacy, Strangis abandoned her and his son in 2005.

Divorced from his first wife by the time he met Melngailis, Strangis convinced her that they would reach the "happily ever after" together. They would face challenges but would overcome them if she did what he told her to do. He talked of strange forces such as The Family, a group of judges that watched everyone and would allow them to pass to the next level of being. She would become immortal – along with her dog Leon. He described himself as a non-human being and that Melngailis was a TBH (tiny blonde human). Melngailis doubted what he told her but went along with it, not wishing to lose out on the "happily ever after" dream.

Strangis travelled a lot, and to prove she was committed to the relationship, he asked Melngailis to send him tens of thousands of dollars. This was a regular occurrence. She took money from the restaurant. If she showed reluctance, he would shout at her and demand she comply. He gave her "cosmic endurance tests", including sending her with a one-way ticket to Rome for 10 days. While she was away in Italy, he had her send $100,000 – leaving no money to pay the restaurant's staff. Melngailis had to borrow to make up for the shortfall.

In January 2015, the restaurant staff walked out after not being paid. Melngailis borrowed $850,000, and the restaurant reopened in April 2015. With the new investors and a restructuring of the business, Melngailis wanted to escape having access to the bank accounts to prevent more money going to Strangis, but this wasn't achieved, and money continued to be drained from the business. With the staff not being paid again, they walked out in July. Strangis and Melngailis took to the road, travelling across the US, eventually reaching Las Vegas, where he spent much time and money gambling.

Strangis asked his wife's family for money, and her mother gave him $400,000. He controlled access to Melngailis, and she was prevented from telling anyone where she was or what was going on. Investors wanted to know.

The couple – who slept in separate rooms – returned to New York for a short period, staying only long enough to collect $60,000 Melngailis had gotten from a friend. The pair then headed south, ending up in Pigeon Forge, Tennessee.

Ironically, it was food of a non-vegan kind that was to deliver the pair into the hands of law enforcement. An order for a takeaway pizza was traced via a credit card transaction to the town. Police then went to a hotel where the couple were staying. Arrested, they were brought back to New York to face charges of grand larceny, criminal tax fraud and scheming to defraud.

Both pleaded guilty. Melngailis received a sentence of five years' probation and four months in Rikers Island prison. Strangis was given probation and a year in jail. They were both ordered to pay restitution.

It was found that between January 2014 and January 2015, Melngailis transferred over $1.6 million from her restaurant business to Strangis. He spent over a million dollars in casinos in Connecticut.

While trying to rebuild her life once out of prison, Melngailis watched a Netflix documentary about Robert Hendy-Freegard. She wondered if she, too, would have ended up under a man's control for ten years. There was no "happily ever after" – the couple divorced in 2018.

TO NO GREAT ACKLOM

Pretending to be a member of the security services is a common theme among our collection of scammers and swindlers. One more to add to the group is Briton Mark Acklom, who broke the heart of a single mum living in England.

Acklom first met Carolyn Woods in January 2012 in Tetbury, Gloucestershire, when, as "Mark Conway", he went into a clothes boutique where she was working. He tried on a few jackets and flirted with her. He was pretending to be a wealthy Swiss banker in the area to buy an old Royal Air Force airfield and restore vintage aircraft. They went on a date the following evening and quickly began a relationship. They started living together; he had swept Woods off her feet. Acklom didn't feel it necessary to inform his new girlfriend that he was already married with children.

After saying he was a banker, Acklom then told Woods he was working for MI6. He was so convincing, Woods later said she thought he was a real-life Jack Bauer from TV show 24. On one occasion, they went to MI6's headquarters in London, and Woods watched as he entered the top secret building past armed guards. Another time, he returned with his arm in a sling, seemingly having been shot while on a mission in Syria.

Woods was the one who proposed marriage; she bought a £6,000 wedding dress. Acklom impressed Woods by telling her he was friends with famous people such as fashion designer Karl Lagerfeld and former US First Lady Hillary Clinton.

Acklom told Woods that when they were married, they'd live in Widcombe Manor House, a Grade I listed building built in the eighteenth century. Along with other properties in Bath, it needed renovation work, and this was going to cost money – money that she provided from life savings and the proceeds from selling her own house.

Once he'd got all Woods's money, Acklom stopped answering her texts and emails. He went on the run, heading to Europe. Woods was devastated and left feeling suicidal after this year-long relationship. She felt he had deliberately isolated her from friends and family, making her a prisoner, something that was a common pattern to others impersonating intelligence or covert operatives. One of Woods's daughters thought Acklom had brainwashed her mother.

Acklom's criminal career had begun in 1991 when still a pupil at the private school Eastbourne College. He was proficient in business studies and was given £15,000 by a teacher to invest on the stock exchange. The teacher never saw his money again.

Acklom stole his father's gold American Express card and spent £11,000 on shopping in Harrods, going to Stringfellows nightclub and staying at the Savoy. Acklom took a girlfriend to the £600-a-night Grand Hotel in Brighton. He ran up a bill of £34,000 in private jets used to take him and his school friends to destinations in Europe.

Always charming and persuasive, Acklom convinced the Leeds Permanent Building Society he was a 25-year-old stockbroker earning over £200,000 a year. They gave him £466,000 to buy a mansion in Dulwich, in south London. The spending spree was halted when Acklom's parents reported him to the police. They had had to sell their house, and his father's business had collapsed as they tried to pay back some of their son's debt.

In 1991, at trial, Acklom faced 124 charges of theft and deception. The judge called him a "wicked conman" and sentenced him to a four-year sentence in a young offenders' institution. He was released in 1993. This brush with the law did not dissuade the privately educated Acklom from committing further crimes.

In 1997, the multi-lingual con artist left the UK and, two years later, in Spain, he was found guilty of financial fraud involving a hotel. This resulted in a three-and-a-half-year jail sentence. In 2004, Acklom was jailed again in Spain for fraud and burglary offences. Two years later and not long out of prison, he was sentenced to 21 months in jail for fraud offences involving pretending to be the owner of a Spanish hotel.

In 2008, Acklom told two Spanish brothers that he was selling three apartments near the Thames in London. He persuaded them to hand over €200,000 as a deposit, despite the fact that he didn't actually own the apartments. It was just another one of his cons.

In 2012, he would meet Carolyn Woods, another person he would take money from. The law caught up with him, and in 2015, he faced trial in Spain for the Thames property scam and was jailed for three years. His own defence lawyer in Spain would later describe his client as "a psychopath" and – reflecting on Acklom's undoubted charm – someone who "could sell smoke – a snake charmer".

In 2016, Acklom was freed after applying for parole. Told to stay in Spain, he went on the run again. The elusive Briton was put on the "most wanted" list, and a European search warrant was issued. Acklom was not averse to moving around Europe and eventually, in 2018, the fugitive was tracked down to a luxury lakeside apartment in Wädenswil, 25 kilometres from Zurich, where, it turned out, he had a Spanish wife and two children. He was living under the guise of being a Spanish business executive. His company was making electronic black box data recorders for autonomous electric cars. According to Acklom, Tesla owner Elon Musk had invested five billion Swiss francs in the company. Swiss investors put in hundreds of thousands of francs, but there was no sign of the technology being produced.

When Swiss police arrived at the apartment, Acklom leaped from a balcony to escape, but a policeman was waiting below just in case he tried to run. After eight months in a Swiss jail – during which he was found guilty of credit card fraud in Switzerland – Acklom was extradited to the UK, where he was sent to prison for over five years for defrauding Carolyn Woods of £300,000.

Woods said in her victim's statement, "My life has indeed been destroyed, and it has only been the love of my two daughters that has prevented me from ending it completely."

Acklom was released from prison in the UK in 2021 but was immediately extradited to Spain so he could serve out the remainder of his fraud sentence there. He was released from prison in Spain in August 2023. A proceeds of crime hearing was scheduled to take place in 2024, to determine Acklom's assets. Woods said, "I'd hoped in the future I might see some of that money, but the chances are very remote indeed. I don't think there is any chance at all."

ATTENTION!

A military romance scam is when a fraudster pretends to be a member of the armed forces to dupe a target they are supposedly in love with out of money. Photographs can be sourced from the internet of a person in uniform, sometimes from stock photo libraries, and these are used to create a profile on dating apps or social media sites like Facebook, Twitter or Instagram.

Most victims of military romance scams are single women aged between 30 and 55. Not all targets are single and looking for a partner. They can be pulled in – or catfished – through curiosity. All victims can find it difficult to resist the attention and persuasive messages that the skilled scammer can produce.

The fraudster contacts the target through messaging. Once a connection is made, they then ask to move the conversation onto a private messaging site like WhatsApp and then delete their original account through which they'd contacted the target.

They might quickly show affection, using terms such as "my dear" or "my love", and tell the intended victim how much they love them and share intimate details of their lives. They are often widowers with children, a situation invented to encourage sympathy. The relationship is built up over weeks and months through frequent interactions.

The fraudster will say they can't do a video call because they are on deployment and involved in military operations. They will keep stringing the target along via texts and private messages. Targets who have respect for those serving in the armed forces are more likely to trust what they are being told by someone apparently in the Army, Navy or Air Force.

Once a strong personal connection has been made, the scammer might ask for money to pay for their travel home on leave or medical treatments for injuries received in combat, or say that they have lost access to their bank accounts. Those combatting such scams are keen to emphasize that serving troops get free travel, free medical care and access to their own money wherever they are in the world.

One genuine soldier who was caught up in the world of military romance frauds is Colonel Daniel Blackmon. Blackmon is an artillery officer in the US Army. He uses social media to promote the work of the Army and has thousands of followers on Twitter (now X) as @UncleRedLeg.

However, his is not the only Twitter account to use the name "Daniel Blackmon" or his photo. Hundreds of fake accounts have been set up using selfies the real Blackmon has posted online. Most actually use his real name and bio as an army colonel, while others use his image but with fictional names. The real Blackmon found out about his imposters in 2014 and reckons his face appears on all of the world's dating sites.

Connie Poindexter first received a message from a Daniel Blackmon in 2021. Since then, she has been contacted by around 15 other Daniel Blackmons. When she confronts the imposters, they tell her that the real Daniel Blackmon is the fake. A single American woman in her 50s called Deborah Colgate was contacted via Facebook by a "Daniel Blackmon" who befriended her. They messaged often, and after a few weeks, "Daniel" told her he wanted to get married as he had separated from his wife. He told Colgate that his son needed surgery for stomach tumours and because he was deployed overseas, he couldn't get access to his own money. Could she lend him a few thousand dollars?

Colgate's daughter worked for a bank and was suspicious. When she searched online, she found the real Blackmon and no money was handed over. To try to counter the scammers, Blackmon tweeted in 2022, "I am happily married, my kids are fine, I don't need money and I am not deployed."

Blackmon is not the only army officer to have been impersonated. Another US Army officer to be the subject of widespread impersonation was General John Campbell, who was the chief commander in Afghanistan in 2015. When Campbell and his staff performed a search online, they found over 700 fake profiles under his name. Among other senior US military commanders to find themselves replicated through multiple profiles was former four-star marine general and secretary of defence under President Trump, James Mattis. The issue was deemed so problematic that the Marine Corps looked to acquire software that would find and then close down any fake profiles.

It is difficult to know how much money has been lost to romance scams as those duped can feel embarrassed and loathe to reveal being conned, but some amounts are known. A woman in the UK who fell for one swindler gave $75,000 in a year. A spokesperson for the US Army's Criminal Investigation Command said in 2014, "The criminals are preying on the emotions and patriotism of their victims."

IMPOSTERS

A major part of many scams is the fraudster not being themselves. They often adopt the identity of someone else, either a real-life person or a fictional one. They may invent a career history or act as if they were present at a highly publicized event.

Frank Abagnale put on the uniform of an airline pilot as part of his activities, while Frenchman Gilbert Chikli pulled on a latex mask and pretended to be a French government minister.

In 2022, it was estimated that Americans lost $2.6 billion in scams featuring imposters, although not all are aiming to profit financially. Tania Head pretended to be a survivor of the 9/11 terror attacks when she wasn't even in New York on that fateful day in September. It is thought she did it to feel part of a community: the community of survivors.

Technology is increasing the way that scammers can attempt to convince victims to hand over their money by being "someone else", and, as always, the intended victims must be on their guard so as not to fall for the imposter.

The next stories all focus on scammers who relied mainly on pretending to be someone else to dupe others, whether it was for money or attention.

GROUNDED

Many children dream of being a pilot, of taking fast jets through the skies, high above the ground. Not all realize these notions, and most settle for more down-to-earth occupations. Some, however, despite not making the grade, say that they did.

One such famous example is Frank Abagnale.

The New Yorker's claims of being a pilot were immortalized in celluloid when a Steven Spielberg film starring Leonardo DiCaprio as Abagnale was released in 2002. *Catch Me If You Can*, inspired by Abagnale's autobiography, was an entertaining movie about a young man who attempted to evade capture from the authorities after donning the uniform of an airline pilot.

While Hollywood is known to take liberties with the truth to make more entertaining movies, in this case, it was building on an "autobiographical" account of a life that seemed to feature events that might not have actually happened. What is true and what is fictional about Abagnale's life is not always clear. Journalists have attempted to dig back into the past to verify the claims he has made, but much remains doubtful.

Some things are accepted as being mostly true.

Born in 1948, Abagnale grew up in a suburb of New York. His dad owned a stationery store, and the 15-year-old Frank ran into trouble when he used the store's credit card to buy items he would then sell on.

When the credit card company noticed an excessive amount of car tyres and batteries being bought in a short time, Frank was found out and sent to reform school.

While still a teenager, he aimed higher – literally. He purchased an American Airlines pilot's uniform with money he had received from cashing stolen blank cheques acquired from a service station. He didn't get far as he was soon convicted of stealing blank bank cheques and sent to prison for two years. After being released, the teenager was sent back to prison for a year for stealing a car in Boston, Massachusetts.

After his release, Abagnale wasn't done with pretending to be a pilot. He impersonated TWA aircrew, but a minister in Baton Rouge, Louisiana, suspected this 20-year-old wasn't a qualified airline pilot. A check with the airline confirmed these suspicions. The police were called, and he was arrested and charged with forging ID documents and also stealing blank cheques. He was given a sentence of supervised probation.

Abagnale fled to Europe but, in September 1969, was arrested in France. He'd stolen a car and was deported back to the US. The lure of the pretend piloting was too much, and he donned a Pan Am uniform. Sometimes his behaviour veered away from the financial into less savoury activities. While pretending to be a doctor, he physically examined young women hoping to become cabin crew. Abagnale was in no position to offer them any sort of employment.

As well as a pilot and a doctor, Abagnale has claimed to have been an attorney general, an operative for the FBI, a police officer and a graduate with a master's in Social Work.

While supposedly acting as a paediatrician in a hospital in the state of Georgia, his usual method to avoid detection was to ask a junior doctor their opinion on a medical case, then respond by saying, "I concur". Abagnale also used his skills in deception to get work as an academic. At a university in Utah, he was a professor of Sociology and was so convincing he was almost given tenure.

In 1970, the serial offender was arrested for trying to pass fake Pan Am payroll cheques. He escaped from jail and, when rearrested in New York, was given 12 years for the forgery plus the escape attempt. In 1974, he was released on parole and once again pretended to be aircrew, and through his "career" got a job at a summer camp. Inevitably, he was arrested – for stealing cameras.

Abagnale changed career and became a security consultant, advising banks on how to avoid being swindled. He was happy to talk publicly about his adventures on television or in public lectures. One tale he related is how he managed to escape capture by the FBI by squirrelling down through the area occupied by a plane's toilet.

Whether it happened or not – or very much else of his story – is up for debate. What is clear is that the man who offered the challenge to catch him if they could, was indeed caught. Several times.

A LONE SURVIVOR

Many survivors of traumatic events are loathe to talk about their experiences. They just wish to carry on with their lives with the horrific experiences parcelled up and left in the past. It is much rarer to find the opposite character type: one who has not suffered trauma but talks as if they have.

One such person was Tania Head. Head claimed to have been in the South Tower of New York's World Trade Center on the morning of 11 September 2001. She related how she was in a meeting on the seventy-eighth floor as an employee of financial company Merrill Lynch when a plane hit the nearby North Tower. She saw people trapped by the fire start to jump from the building. When the second plane hit the South Tower, she had to crawl through the horror of the burning building to get to the stairs, past the remains of those who had died, including her own assistant, who had been decapitated.

One dying man handed her his wedding ring, and she promised to deliver it to his widow. At one point, a man called Welles Crowther beat out the flames as her clothes burned and showed her the way out.

She made it down and then out alive to find that her fiancé David Suarez, who worked in the North Tower, had not survived. Crowther, known as "the man in the red bandana" and who had saved several others, also perished.

Head spent a week in hospital, where her injuries were treated, including a severely damaged arm. Once recovered, she heavily involved herself as part of a survivor's community, helping to gain public attention for their stories, which were often forgotten. She became the president of the World Trade Center Survivors' Network and helped to give it a large public profile. Membership grew to over a thousand. Head helped organize events and managed to secure public funding.

She gave tours of Ground Zero, showing dignitaries like New York Mayors Rudolph Giuliani and Michael Bloomberg around the site. She appeared on TV and at conferences to share her experiences. The story she told was inspiring; how she had overcome such personal tragedy and continued to live a full, worthwhile life.

As the sixth anniversary of the 9/11 attacks approached, *The New York Times* wanted to run a story on survivors. As part of their background checks, doubts began to appear around Head's story. Merrill Lynch denied she had ever worked there. David's family had no recollection of him ever speaking about his fiancée. Head had claimed to have studied at Harvard and Stanford, but both universities had no record of her. Furthermore, Head's own story was not always consistent. For example, David was sometimes a fiancé and, other times, a husband. A charity she claimed to have set up in her fiancé's honour never existed.

The truth was that she was not Tania Head, but Alicia Esteve Head, a Spanish woman who was not in New York or even the US on that fateful day. She was studying at a

Spanish business school. The scars on her arms were not from a terrorist attack but from a car accident.

The survivor's network, upset and angry at being fooled, disassociated itself from Head, stripping her of the presidency. Why she pretended to be a 9/11 survivor is not known. It was not to make money – Head donated money to the group – but perhaps it was the lure of the attention or to be part of a community of shared experience. Despite her duplicity and the resulting anguish, some survivors were still thankful that she gave their experiences a public voice.

Head isn't the only person to pretend to be a survivor of a terrorist incident. On the evening of 13 November 2015, Islamist terrorists attacked Paris. They detonated bombs and fired assault rifles at civilians at the Stade de France sports stadium, the Bataclan concert venue and several restaurants and bars, killing 130 people. One of the bars was Le Carillon.

Paris resident Alexandra Damien said she was at Le Carillon when two of her friends were killed. She had a scar from one of the attackers' Kalashnikov rifles. She registered as a victim and was awarded €20,000 from a fund for victims of the attacks. Damien attended therapy sessions for survivors.

It turned out that the 32-year-old was planning to go to the bar that night but had changed her mind. She woke early the next morning to find dozens of missed calls from those concerned about her safety and who didn't know about her change of plans. Damien went to see the tributes left at the bar, where she was interviewed by the media, expressing her sadness and shock at the loss of two of her friends. Then, she added that she had been there when the shooting started.

When the truth was revealed, Damien was sent to prison for six months for fraud and perjury. The scars on her arm had come from a kite surfing accident. Damien said at her trial, "I come to ask for forgiveness. This is the biggest mistake of my life."

She wasn't the only one to lie about her involvement in these attacks.

A 49-year-old woman fraudulently claimed to be in the Bataclan and faked a receipt for a concert ticket. She received €25,000 in compensation and four and a half years in jail for the deception. An ambulance driver was sent to prison for six months for also saying he was at the Bataclan when he wasn't even in Paris at the time.

FOR WHOM THE BELLE TOLLS

Once cancer sufferers have gotten over the shock of their diagnosis, they move onto the stage of looking for treatment and a cure for this terrible disease. If conventional medicine doesn't prove to be successful, alternative methods are often tried by those desperate to live.

In 2013, a young Australian woman called Belle Gibson claimed that her own brain cancer was being successfully treated through alternative therapies, exercise and a restrictive, plant-based diet free of gluten and dairy. She used oxygen therapy and colonic irrigation. The conventional treatments of chemotherapy and radiotherapy had been carried out but had failed. She had been living with this terminal disease for five years despite only being given four months to live.

Gibson gained a huge following on Instagram as a wellness guru and was one of the first super-influencers. Her 200,000 followers were keen to follow and live their own "best lives".

Aged 21, she launched the world's first wellness mobile phone app: *The Whole Pantry*. It was hugely successful, being downloaded 200,000 times in the first month. Apple planned to include it in their Apple Watch. An associated cookbook published by Penguin followed. Processed foods and dairy products were not allowed.

In December 2014, Australian *Elle* magazine named her "The Most Inspiring Woman You've Met This Year", while Cosmopolitan gave her an award for being a "Fun, Fearless Female".

Then, Gibson announced that the cancer had spread and now affected her blood, uterus, kidneys, spleen and liver. She still looked to be in glowing health, and some journalists began to have doubts about the veracity of her claims. They looked into Gibson's story, but she didn't produce any evidence to back up her claims.

Gibson then said she did have brain cancer, but the other ones were falsely diagnosed. She then came clean and admitted to having invented all her cancer diagnoses. She said in a magazine interview, "None of it's true. I don't want forgiveness." This wasn't the first time she had claimed serious ill health. Several years prior to this, Gibson had supposedly suffered strokes and undergone heart surgery several times. She had also claimed that during one operation, she had died but was resuscitated.

In March 2015, further trouble arose when it was discovered that charity donations she had promised had not materialized. Out of the AUD $300,000 claimed to have been donated from the app and book proceeds, only around AUD $7,000 had been paid. *The Whole Pantry* had earned her AUD $440,000.

The app was removed from Apple's app store, and the book was taken off Penguin's list. In 2017, Gibson was fined AUD $410,000 for making false claims and misleading the public. When the fine (plus interest and penalties taking it up to half a million Australian dollars) was not paid – Gibson claimed to only have AUD $5,000 to her name – police raided her house to seize assets.

She had gone on holiday to Bali and Africa but, in court, was unable to say who had paid for these trips.

The media who had featured Gibson were criticized for not properly doing background checks. Gibson was also criticized for endangering cancer victims who might have turned away from proven conventional treatments.

She subsequently disappeared from public view and was rumoured to have converted to Islam. In her book, she had written, "I was empowering myself to save my own life through nutrition, patience, determination, and love."

CON KING OF HOLLYWOOD

Hollywood is the capital of the US film industry. For decades, it's where aspiring actors, writers and technicians have gone to try and make it in the most glamorous of workplaces. Due to the structure of the movie-making sector, most of the workers are freelance, employed on a short-term, film-by-film basis. A film executive or producer who needs make-up artists, stunt artists, physical trainers, scriptwriters or cinematographers will contact them and get their agreement to take part in whatever project they've got.

This was the method used by a person known as the "Hollywood Con Queen". She would contact prospective gig workers in the guise of powerful women, well-known in Tinseltown, such as Kathleen Kennedy (president of Lucasfilm, started by *Star Wars* originator George Lucas); Amy Pascal (Sony Pictures chairperson); Stacey Snider (former chair and CEO of 20th Century Fox and DreamWorks, and chair of Universal Pictures) and Deborah Snyder (co-producer of films such as *Watchmen*, *Man of Steel* and *Wonder Woman*).

The recipients of these calls were those desperate to make their mark in the industry – usually young, male and without extensive CVs. They responded positively to these opportunities offered by such influential luminaries of the movie world.

The Queen would use Skype – but with the camera off – and offer candidates the chance to travel to Indonesia, where major movies were being going to be made. These movies had titles like *The Master* and *Gotham City Sirens*, and the candidates' involvement would be their big break into the industry.

However, after paying for their own flights to Indonesia, when they arrived, the workers-turned-victims never got anywhere near a film set. They would be told of delays and other excuses why they weren't starting to work – or getting paid. The victims would have to use their own money – for their driver, for a tour guide, for translation services, for photo permits, or a range of other spurious outlays. The money would be collected by the Queen's accomplices, who were part of this catfishing operation. Although promised reimbursement, the victims never saw a cent.

In 2020, the suspected real identity of the Queen was revealed. Despite the gender being suggested by the pseudonym, an Indonesian man living in the UK called Hargobind Punjabi Tahilramani was identified as the source of the phoney calls. He was arrested and accused of wire fraud, conspiracy to commit wire fraud and identity theft when scamming over 300 victims for over $1 million. It was discovered that the man had spent time in prison in Indonesia for saying there was a bomb in the US Embassy.

In June 2023, after two years of legal action, his extradition to the US was approved by a British judge. The judge said at the hearing, "I found him to be dishonest and manipulative."

DEATH OF A PRINCESS

While many young girls dream of being a princess, most leave these thoughts behind on reaching adulthood. They do not cling to these fantasies into old age.

In 1917, Russia was torn apart by revolution and civil war. The royal family, which had ruled for centuries, was removed from power. The Tsar, Nicholas II, his wife Alexandra and their five children were held captive by Bolshevik forces for over a year before being assassinated in July 1918. They were shot and stabbed to death. Their bodies were then thrown into a mine before being moved to a forest. The Bolsheviks took pains to try to make sure they could not be identified, using grenades and sulphuric acid in an attempt to destroy their remains.

In the ensuing years, the Soviet Union's reluctance to acknowledge the Romanovs' fate allowed intrigue and mystery. Among these was the idea that the Tsar's youngest daughter, 17-year-old Anastasia, had escaped. With rumours of the Romanov fortune being held outside Russia, there were potential financial rewards for anyone who could prove they were a surviving family member.

One such claimant emerged in Germany in the 1920s. The woman said she had escaped being murdered by the Bolsheviks alongside the rest of the royal family through the actions of a sympathetic Bolshevik soldier.

The woman, who called herself Anna Tschaikovsky, found her claims to be a Romanov were met with scepticism and also belief. Anastasia's nanny and her tutor visited her and averred she was not who she said she was. For one thing, Tschaikovsky couldn't speak Russian.

Tschaikovsky did have a facial resemblance to the Tsar's youngest daughter, and while there were sceptics, others believed her, with a series of supporters providing her with accommodation. These included members of the Danish and Bavarian aristocracy. One visitor to Tschaikovsky was Tatiana Melnik (née Botkin), whose father was the Tsar's doctor who was killed by the Bolsheviks alongside the Tsar and his family. Melnik knew Anastasia and thought the childlike woman she encountered was indeed her.

Ernest Louis, the Grand Duke of Hesse whose sister Alexandra had married the Tsar in 1894, was suspicious. He instigated an investigation which revealed that the woman claiming to be his niece was, in fact, Franziska Schanzkowska, a young Polish factory worker with a history of mental health issues.

Schanzkowska had been incarcerated in an asylum following a suspected suicide attempt in Berlin in 1920. (While in the asylum, a fellow inmate had claimed she was another of the Tsar's daughters, Tatiana, although these claims were rubbished by those who saw her, including a former lady-in-waiting to the Tsarina.)

After the Grand Duke of Hesse had exposed her as a fraud in Germany, Schanzkowska moved to the US and adopted the name of Anna Anderson to avoid press attention. Here, at one point, the composer and pianist Sergei Rachmaninoff paid for her to stay at the luxurious Garden City Hotel on Long Island. She was a celebrity in New York society but returned to Germany in 1931 after erratic behaviour saw her being taken into a psychiatric hospital in New York state.

Schanzkowska moved back to the US in 1968, where she was to live for the rest of her life. Her claims, unsuccessfully pursued through the courts for decades, were finally given up in 1970. The woman who claimed to be of royal blood died in 1984. She was cremated, thus removing any opportunity for DNA analysis.

The mystery of what happened to the Tsar's family continued until the collapse of the Soviet Union, and the use of DNA provided the much-anticipated answer. The remains of five of the Tsar's family had been found in the 1970s, but it was not until after the collapse of the Soviet Union in the 1990s that their remains were exhumed. Where were the other two? Had Anastasia escaped murder all those years before?

It was not until 2007 that the graves of two children were found. Through several tests, DNA from all the remains, Schanzkowska's hair and a tissue sample from a medical procedure when she was alive were compared. The Tsarina Alexandra's great-nephew, Prince Philip (the husband of Britain's Queen Elizabeth II), also gave a blood sample to aid identification.

When the results were announced they were conclusive: the remains were confirmed as Romanov. This meant Franziska Schanzkowska could not be Anastasia. All the members of the Tsar's close family had died a century before. If there was a fortune hidden away, it remains so.

WHO'S SOROKIN NOW?

Frank Sinatra sang of how if you could succeed in New York, you had what it takes to make it anywhere. One young Russian woman called Anna Sorokin set out to New York to "make it" but instead only made it to jail.

As a teenager, she had left Russia with her family and gone west to live in Germany. She spent some time in London and Paris before arriving in New York in 2013. While in Paris, she started using the name "Anna Delvey". Once in New York, Sorokin claimed to be a German heiress, with her father's wealth coming from the oil industry, making solar panels, being a diplomat or via antiques, depending on who she told. Sorokin behaved as if she had large amounts of money, wearing designer clothes, staying in boutique hotels, insisting on paying for meals and giving hotel staff hundred-dollar tips, but, strangely, the money wasn't always available to pay for this lifestyle. Bills for meals, flights or hotel rooms went unpaid. Friends would pay on the promise of being paid back. Sorokin claimed she had tens of millions of dollars, but it was held in trust in Switzerland, and she couldn't access it. She applied for bank loans, but staff were suspicious, at one point noticing she claimed to be German while her passport stated she was born in Russia.

Loving the good things in life, she once stayed in a Manhattan hotel and ran up a $30,000 bill. This was paid off via fraudulent cheques. At times, when funds were not available, she would demand to sleep on a friend's couch. She hosted her own birthday party at a Soho restaurant, but when the owners rang one of her friends to ask for her contact details as the bill hadn't been paid, the friend realized that perhaps Sorokin didn't have the money she claimed.

When in Paris, Sorokin had interned at a fashion magazine, but once she had arrived in the Big Apple, she aimed higher in the fashion world.

The Anna Delvey Foundation would be a private, members-only club with art studios, pop-up shops, restaurants, bars and event spaces. Exhibitions by artists Damien Hirst, Jeff Koons and Tracey Emin would bring a large amount of cachet from the art world. The venture would take up all six floors of a historic Manhattan building called the Church Missions House, situated on the corner of Park Avenue and 22nd Street.

This would need money, lots of money – in the region of $25 million.

In November and December 2016, Sorokin had tried to secure loans from banks in New York for over $20 million to pay for her foundation. She submitted false bank statements showing her supposed wealth: $60 million. When one of the New York banks wanted to verify her assets in Switzerland, Sorokin abandoned the plan. She was able to access $55,000 of the $100,000 received for an overdraft to pay for legal expenses and due diligence during the loan application. When this money ran out – spent in a month – she used fake cheques to obtain $70,000.

During her time in New York, Sorokin had befriended Rachel DeLoache Williams, who worked as a photo editor at *Vanity Fair* magazine. In May 2017, Sorokin invited her personal trainer Kacy Duke, Williams and a videographer on a trip to Morocco. The videographer was to film a documentary on the preparations for the New York Foundation.

They stayed in a five-star hotel, but when Sorokin couldn't produce a working credit card, she insisted that Williams pay the bill. The $62,000 bill. Sorokin then asked Duke, who had to return home early due to food poisoning, to pay for her flight home – first class.

Back in New York, Sorokin was evicted from two hotels for non-payment of her bills. Time was running out – she was being investigated by the New York district attorney. In July 2017, she faced misdemeanour charges of theft of services for the two hotels she stiffed.

In October 2017, she was arrested on a visit to California, having paid for the trip by depositing bad cheques. Rachel DeLoache Williams assisted in the arrest by finding out where Sorokin was and informing the police.

Back in New York, the former "heiress" faced charges of grand larceny and attempted grand larceny, as well as the misdemeanour charges. In March 2019, Sorokin appeared in court in New York. Always keen to dress to impress, each day in court was marked by a new outfit. When on one day her outfit had not arrived, she refused to enter the court until ordered to by the judge.

Found guilty, Sorokin was given a prison sentence of four to nine years, fined and ordered to pay restitution to some of those she owed money. A deal with Netflix provided $320,000 towards the restitution. The streaming platform produced a nine-part drama series called *Inventing Anna*, starring Julia Garner as Sorokin. When it was broadcast in February 2022, it was Netflix's most watched programme.

Sorokin served four years in prison. She said in 2022 that she was keen to move away from being portrayed as "the fake heiress". She stated, "I'd love to be given an opportunity for people not to just dismiss me as a quote-unquote scammer."

WOLF PACK OF LIES

The Second World War was the source of amazing stories of fortitude amid the horror and carnage. As well as soldiers, sailors and airmen, these inspiring tales came from civilians such as resistance fighters or those who sheltered others in danger. When an incredible story came from a woman who had been a young girl during the conflict, it quickly gained attention.

Misha Defonseca was living in the US when she first told her story. She related what happened when she was a young Jewish girl, aged seven, living in Belgium. One day in 1941, her father failed to pick her up from school. He never turned up, and she was fostered by a Catholic family who changed her name to Monique de Wael. She found out her mother and father had been taken by the Nazis and deported to the camps in Germany.

Misha (now Monique) determined to walk to Germany to find her parents. She set off on her own through the woods. Alone, she became friendly with a lone wolf and was then accepted by the pack, who looked after her.

Misha kept walking for months. At one point, she had to kill a Nazi soldier to survive. She spent time in the Warsaw Ghetto. She eventually spent four years evading the Nazis and certain death for one born a Jew.

In the US, a publisher called Jane Daniel saw the potential of Misha's story as someone who had escaped the Holocaust. When the book came out, Disney and Oprah Winfrey also saw the human interest in this extraordinary tale of endurance. Disney optioned the film rights, and Misha was booked to appear on Oprah's book club. A sequence of her interacting with wolves was filmed. Misha's book was translated into 18 languages, and a film of her exploits was made in France.

Defonseca then filed a lawsuit against her publisher for unpaid royalties and a return of copyright. Defonseca won and was awarded $22.5 million. Her publisher did not have that money. The deals with Disney and Oprah Winfrey were abandoned.

When going through her files, Daniel noticed something strange. In bank documents, Defonseca had given her mother's surname despite it being something she said she didn't recall. On top of this, there were inconsistencies in the book, such as the surname of her wartime foster family being different in the American and French versions. In the former, she was given the surname "de Wael" and in the latter, "Valle". The French version would be read in Belgium, which raised suspicions that the change was made in order to prevent anyone delving into her history there.

Further investigations in Belgium showed that a Catholic girl called Monique de Wael attended school in Brussels in 1943, two years after Defonseca said she was not there and out in the countryside evading the Nazis.

In 2008, Defonseca came clean and admitted her story was fiction. She said, "It's not the true reality, but it is my reality." It turned out that the historical reality was that her father was part of the Belgian resistance. He was arrested and, during interrogation by the Gestapo, he gave the Nazis the names of other resistance members, who were then also arrested.

Both parents later died in Nazi concentration camps. Defonseca's father's name was removed from a war memorial. She grew up labelled as "The Traitor's Daughter". In 2014, a court ordered Defonseca to pay her publisher back the $22.5 million.

MOMMIE DEAREST

The film *Psycho* depicts a mentally ill man who is tortured by the presence of his dead mother and who murders those who come to his motel. When Norman Bates kills his victims, he dresses as his deceased parent.

New York actress Irene Pruskin died in 2003, aged 77. She owned a property in Brooklyn for which she had ceded the deed to her son Thomas Parkin in the 1990s. Parkin was unable to make the mortgage payments for the $2.2 million brownstone apartment, and it was sold at a foreclosure auction. Parkin took out a lawsuit against the new owner in his mother's name, claiming it was invalid since she was still alive.

When Parkin asked investigators from the Brooklyn District Attorney's office to come to his mother's house to talk about the case, instead of a woman in her 70s, officials found a man in his 40s impersonating a woman in her 70s.

Parkin's performance failed immediately. Despite a blond wig, heavy makeup, a woman's cardigan and using an oxygen tank, the DA's staff saw right through it. A spokesman for the DA said, "He fooled no one." They had gone along to the meeting with a fairly good idea that things were not as Parkin had claimed: they had a photograph of Parkin's mother's grave. When his mother had died, Parkin had given false information to the undertaker so that her death wouldn't be registered properly. To all intents and purposes, she was still alive.

In May 2012, Parkin was given a jail sentence for a minimum of 13 years for mortgage fraud, grand larceny, forgery, perjury and criminal impersonation. He had been claiming his mother's social security and rent subsidy money for six years (taking in over $100,000).

Parkin, who told detectives, "I held my mother when she was dying and breathed in her last breath, so I am my mother", was sent to a male prison.

PERSONAL BRANDON

The thought may sometimes cross an adult's head of what it would be like to go back to school. Notions of the "best days of your life" may be a welcome refuge from the stresses and strains of current life. The concept of an older person returning to school has been the subject of entertaining movies like *Freaky Friday* and *Peggy Sue Got Married*. These were fictional, but what happened at a Scottish high school in the 1990s was real.

In August 1993, the new intake of fifth years started at Bearsden Academy in the north of Glasgow, Scotland's biggest city. Among them was a tall, thin pupil called Brandon Lee. Some of his classmates remarked that his name was the same as the recently deceased Hollywood actor, who had died in an accident on a film set.

Some of them thought Lee looked older than the rest of the 16- and 17-year-olds who made up the fifth year. He was perhaps a student teacher.

Lee's accent stuck out, explained by his being from Canada. His mother, an opera singer, had died in a car crash, and he'd been sent to Scotland to live with his grandmother.

Lee was 16 but was more mature than most of his classmates and had great confidence and general knowledge. He could also drive a car. Lee took a leading role in the school musical *South Pacific*. He invited his fellow pupils to his house or into the city centre to go to record shops or the cinema.

When his exams came, he gained five A-grade Higher awards. These results earned him a place at the University of Dundee to study medicine, but once there, he left after a term, saying he couldn't continue with his studies because his grandmother had died. Afterwards, Lee went on a foreign holiday to Tenerife with some of his former classmate friends. It was there that the deceit started to unravel when one of those friends told her parents, who informed the Academy that Lee was not who he said he was.

The news broke big. There was huge media interest in this remarkable tale.

"Brandon Lee" was really Brian MacKinnon, a man who was 30 when he went back to the school he'd studied at years before. MacKinnon had left Bearsden Academy in 1980 and gone to the University of Glasgow to study medicine. He was thrown off the course after failing his exams.

The years went by, but he always wanted to be a doctor. As there was an age limit of 30 for studying medicine, he came up with a ruse of a new high-school-age persona called Brandon Lee, who, after gaining his high school qualifications, could apply to medical school.

When the story broke, it was revealed that his grandmother, whose death had led him to drop out of studying at Dundee, was not in fact dead – she was his mother.

No one at Bearsden Academy had cottoned on to the real identity of this pupil, even teachers who had taught him a decade previously. Remarkably, there was a real classmate called Brian MacKinnon in Lee's class whom he had befriended. Lee almost responded when the form teacher called their names for the register. The ruse could have been rumbled far earlier.

In *My Old School*, a documentary made about his story released in 2022, MacKinnon said, "The thing you have to do if you really want to prevail is do the unimaginable." He is said to still live in Bearsden near the school he attended. Twice.

GUESS WHO'S COMING TO DINNER?

Being a child of a famous personality can have its pitfalls, but it can also be a ticket to easier restaurant reservations, invitations to special events and a host of other nice things in life. One man who faced several hardships was David Hampton. He wasn't the child of anyone famous – but he pretended to be.

One night in 1983, Hampton and a friend attempted to get into New York's famous Studio 54 nightclub. When they were refused entry, they came up with a ruse. David would pretend to be the son of Oscar-winning actor Sidney Poitier and his friend would be Gregory Peck's son. On returning to the nightclub in a limo, they were ushered straight inside.

Hampton was the son of an attorney in Buffalo, New York state, and had wanted to escape as it had nothing there for him. He once said, "No one who lived there was glamorous or fabulous or outrageously talented." He moved to New York aged 19 following a chequered career at college in Buffalo, where he had been arrested for stealing money from a fellow student.

After his initial success, Hampton continued to pretend to be Poitier's son (the actor didn't actually have a son, he had six daughters). He would tell aspiring actors there could be parts for them in his father's movies.

While dining out, he would tell the restaurant staff he was waiting for his father to arrive. When Poitier Sr didn't turn up, the restaurant would take care of the bill for the son of such a big movie star.

Hampton would say he was a friend of other famous people's children. He would land at the door of the likes of Calvin Klein or Melanie Griffith and make up some excuse that would mean they would take him in for the night. Or two. He was happy to receive food, money or clothes. One time, he managed to secure a bed, some money and clothes by saying he had been mugged and had lost his Harvard thesis entitled "Injustices in the Criminal Justice System".

The people who took him in were Osborn and Inger Elliott. Osborn Elliott was dean of Columbia University's Graduate School of Journalism, a former editor of *Newsweek* magazine and deputy mayor of New York. Hampton claimed he was friends with their daughter. The Elliotts' generosity was rewarded by Hampton sneaking in a boyfriend. When they contacted their daughter, she told her parents she didn't know any David Poitier.

Hampton was shown the door, but this wasn't the end of it. Osborn Elliott went to the police, and they found others who had opened their doors and then lost money to him. Hampton was ordered to repay $4,500 to those he had duped, but when he failed to do so, was given a jail term. He spent 21 months in state prison.

When the Elliotts told a friend their tale of being conned by a young man, he thought it might make good material for a play. *Six Degrees of Separation* by John Guare opened on

Broadway in 1990. It was nominated for four Tony awards and was later made into a movie starring Will Smith as "Paul", a young Black man claiming to be the son of Sidney Poitier.

When Hampton heard of the play being produced, he returned to New York to grab some of the publicity. He took things further: suing John Guare and those responsible for the play for $100 million as the play was based on his real life. He did not win his case, the judge ruling that those who break the law shouldn't be rewarded and that someone's personality does not have the same legal protection as trademarks or copyrights.

Hampton did not take the legal decision well, harassing Guare and issuing violent threats. During one recorded phone call, he said he would do something "so that you won't be able to walk on stage and accept any awards". Hampton was acquitted of harassing Guare, his lawyer successfully arguing it was just the sort of rough speech you got in a city.

Hampton continued his charming, grifting ways. In 1990, he was ejected from the campus of New York University for attempting to find a place to stay by telling students he had written the hit play.

He kept up his duplicitous ways across the US, adopting various pseudonyms. In 2001, he went on a date with a man called Peter Bedevian. "Hampton-Montilio" – as he was that night – managed to get his date to give him a thousand dollars for concert tickets and then disappeared into the night. Despite pressing charges to get his thousand dollars back, Bedevian said it was one of the best dates he'd had.

When Hampton died of AIDS in 2003, aged 39, *The New York Times* headline stated, "He conned the society crowd but died alone."

THE GREAT WALDO IMPOSTER

Ferdinand "Fred" Demara earned the title of "The Great Imposter" due to a packed career of impersonation. At times, he was Joseph C. Cyr, Dr Robert Linton French, Martin Godgart, Dr Cecil Boyce Hamann, Anthony Ingolia, Ben W. Jones, Frank Kingston and Jefferson B. Thorne. Some were real people, while others were his own creations.

Demara was born in 1921 in Massachusetts. When the Great Depression hit, his family were forced to move because his father's business had gone bust. Aged 16, Demara – known to his friends as Fred – ran away from home to begin what he felt was a mission from God to do good.

He began a remarkable and varied career in many different locations.

His desire to serve God saw him spend two years in a Rhode Island monastery where his inability to keep quiet meant he was asked to leave the silent environment. He felt the menial jobs he was given at his next port of call, a religious retreat in Canada, were beneath him, and he left to teach in Massachusetts. After falling out with the brother superior, he stole a car and left for Boston.

In 1941, he joined the US Army on an impulse but soon regretted it and went absent without leave. He didn't go empty-handed, taking the identity of a fellow soldier: Anthony Ingolia.

His fake identify, was rumbled at an abbey in Iowa, and Demara quickly left. He was advised by his father to turn himself in for desertion but, never one to take sensible advice, plotted his own course and enlisted in the Navy, doing so just weeks after Pearl Harbor. Not enjoying life on a warship in the Atlantic, he applied to be a medical corpsman. He excelled but was not given advanced training. Feeling snubbed, he faked papers showing a background suitable enough to gain a commission as an officer but realized he had exposed himself. He left his time in uniform by faking his suicide.

Out of uniform again, Demara became Dr Robert Linton French, a psychologist who had left the Navy after seeing the futility of war. He went to an abbey in Kentucky, but Dr French wasn't able to resist eating or talking and was quietly told to try another way of serving God.

Still as French, the irrepressible character tried a monastery in Arkansas, but the abbot suspected his documents were forged. He left. "Dr French" did not give up and presented himself at several other religious centres. At one in Illinois, he converted to Catholicism despite being one from birth. At another, in Milwaukee, he departed after a dispute over his cooking abilities.

In the autumn of 1945, Dr French was appointed dean of the School of Philosophy at Gannon College, Erie, Pennsylvania. He gave lectures in courses such as "abnormal psychology". He also published a booklet on raising children (he didn't have any). An accusation over his profligate spending led to his departure.

On the road again, Dr French ended up at a Hospitallers' institution in California to find there was no requirement for a psychologist, as it was a home for the elderly, not a medical hospital. While he was adept at adopting personas, he sometimes made mistakes which could have given him away. While at this institution, "Doctor" French was asked about his clothing. It turned out the jackets he was wearing were not correct for a medical doctor but more appropriate for a barber! French was soon on the road again.

On his way west, Dr French had stopped off to see a bishop in Salt Lake City and made sure to lift some of the bishop's official stationery, which was used to provide a letter of testimony, handy for securing future positions.

His next stop was in Washington at a Benedictine educational institution, where, after befriending the local sheriff, he was appointed an honorary deputy sheriff, gaining the right to carry a gun and have a siren on his car.

This wasn't enough to prevent the past from catching up with him: Demara was arrested by the FBI for desertion in time of war, an offence which could result in the death penalty. Throwing himself on the mercy of the court, he avoided the death penalty and was given six years in jail, of which he served 18 months, being released early for good behaviour.

Once outside, he was no longer Dr French, but back to being Demara. For a while, at least. He adopted the persona of Cecil Boyce Hamann and went to study law in Boston, but he found it boring. And, as often in the past, Demara became someone else: Brother John Payne, at a religious teaching order in Maine, where he arrived in 1950. He said he was a zoologist with a PhD. He had big plans and set up a new college, but when overlooked as rector, he stole a car and departed.

It was while at this order that the seeds of Demara's most famous exploit were sewn. He met a Canadian surgeon called Joseph C. Cyr and took his birth certificate, medical licence and other documents. In 1951, Demara joined the Royal Canadian Navy as Joseph Cyr. After a period in a hospital at Halifax, he was assigned to a destroyer, the *Cayuga*, which was soon sailing towards the Korean War. Demara was given the responsible role of being the ship's medical officer despite no relevant medical training. Claiming a photographic memory, Demara read up all the medical manuals he could get. He didn't find all he needed in them, however. When tasked with removing an infected tooth from the ship captain's mouth, Demara gave him so much novocaine the captain's head went numb.

One day, a group of 19 wounded Korean soldiers were taken out to the ship. Demara summoned his courage, downed some rum and forced himself to treat the soldiers. With no option, he operated on the most seriously wounded and managed to extract a bullet from near to one patient's heart. All the soldiers lived.

His efforts were rewarded with widespread publicity. When the real Joseph Cyr found out, the game was up. To save the embarrassment of having recruited a non-medical "doctor", the Canadian Navy quietly discharged him, and he returned to the US.

Demara later sold his life story to *Life* magazine, giving most of the $2,500 fee to his parents. The publicity made any future impersonating much harder, but this didn't prevent

Demara from trying. He worked in various locations in various roles, including as an accountant, prison warden, teacher, pastor and chaplain. Although he fell short in his aim of doing good and serving God, there is no doubt that Demara tried and, if nothing else, provided entertainment for anyone hearing his story. Demara's exploits were perfect for Hollywood, and Tony Curtis played this great imposter in 1961's *The Great Imposter*.

BOURDIN OF PROOF

When word came in October 1997 that Nicholas Barclay had been found, his family were overjoyed. The family of the American teenager had longed for news since he went missing in June 1994 after playing basketball near his home in San Antonio, Texas.

When his older half-sister, Carey Gibson, asked where in Texas he had been located, she was told, no, he was in Spain, Europe. Leaving the US for the first time, she flew to Spain and greeted her lost brother. The Spanish authorities had doubts about whether it really was him, but these were dispelled when he was able to identify family photographs brought over by Gibson. He was issued an American passport.

Nicholas Barclay arrived in the US and was warmly welcomed by his family, including his mother, Beverly Dollarhide. When he walked off the plane, Barclay was wearing dark glasses, a scarf around his neck, and two baseball hats. He was quiet and didn't say much. When he did speak, it was with a French accent.

When questioned, Barclay explained his absence by claiming to have been kidnapped by military figures and then sexually abused and tortured for three years, along with other children.

In Texas, one of those who had suspicions all was not as it seemed was private investigator Charlie Parker. He had been hired by current affairs TV show *Hard Copy* to secure an interview with Barclay. During the taping of the interview, Parker thought it strange that Barclay's eyes were a different colour in a family photograph than in person. Later, Parker compared the shape of Barclay's ears to that in the photograph. There were differences in shape. He was convinced the boy was not the real Barclay.

The FBI were also doubtful, noticing the returned child had dark stubble and appeared to be older than 16, but the family had accepted him as their missing boy and refused to allow any doubt or examination through DNA checks.

A child psychiatrist, when he spoke to Barclay, felt something wasn't right: Barclay didn't exhibit any signs of experiencing the extreme trauma that he had supposedly suffered. He was also unable to speak English without a foreign accent, as he should have, having been raised in the US. Barclay had explained his accent away by saying he was forbidden from speaking English for three years.

These doubts were confirmed when fingerprint and DNA tests proved that the person at the centre of all this interest was not Nicholas Barclay. He was a 23-year-old Frenchman called Frédéric Bourdin. Bourdin had sourced details of the missing American teenager and had taken on his persona.

Barclay had blonde hair, blue eyes, a gap in his front teeth and tattoos. Bourdin dyed his hair, said that he'd had his eye colour changed through chemical eye drops by those who kidnapped him, and arranged to have the tattoos added. He did have a gap in his teeth.

The FBI received information on Bourdin's past. He had been raised by his grandparents in Nantes after his mother had given him up when he was only two years old. He ended up in children's homes but had run away when a teenager. Bourdin had created many false identities of different nationalities, such as Shadjan Raskovic (Bosnian), Thomas Wilson (Australian), Shedgin Gueyere (Mexican) and Benjamin Kent (British). He would travel through Europe and then present himself at a youth shelter, pretending to be a juvenile – looking for somewhere that would take care of him.

Bourdin was sentenced to prison for six years for perjury and fraudulently obtaining a passport. After serving his sentence, he was deported back to Europe in 2003.

Back there, the man the press had nicknamed "The Chameleon" resumed his impersonating, pretending to be a missing 14-year-old French schoolboy called Léo Balley, then a Spanish schoolboy called Rubén Sánchez Espinoza and then a 15-year-old Spanish orphan called Francisco Hernandez Fernandez.

The real Nicholas Barclay remains unlocated.

A PRINCETON
AMONG THIEVES

Scotsman Brian MacKinnon wasn't unique in wanting to go back to school while he was too old to do so. In the US, a man called James Hogue faked his way into high school and university. Hogue was born in 1959 and grew up in Kansas, graduating from high school in 1977, where he was known as a good athlete.

That summer, he attended the University of Wyoming, joining the cross-country running team. In his second year, he dropped out after a disappointing performance, finishing two hundred and twenty-sixth out of 250 in a 10,000-metre regional race.

Hogue went on to the University of Texas at Austin but left without graduating. His next try at education was in 1985, when, as "Jay Huntsman", he started attending not a university but a high school: Palo Alto High School in California.

Huntsman had wanted to enrol at Stanford University, but as the entry requirements included being a high school graduate, he had to go to the nearby high school first. The school's principal queried his age, thinking he looked older than the typical high school student. As an athlete, he had impressed – as would be expected by an athlete seven to eight years older than his competitors – by winning a cross-country race. He surprised onlookers by not accepting his prize.

Huntsman stated he was from San Diego and that both his parents had been killed in a car crash in Bolivia. A reporter who was at the cross-country race had his suspicions. He looked into this athlete's background and found there had indeed been a Jay Huntsman from San Diego, but he had died when he was only a few days old. When his school was alerted, and the reporter published the story, the police were called. Huntsman admitted he was, in fact, James Hogue and left the school.

He encountered the police a few months later, being arrested for forging cheques. These charges were subsequently dropped.

Hogue next appeared in Colorado and claimed to be a professor in bioengineering at Stanford. He secured a summer job at a sports training camp, instructing runners and cyclists. When a check was made, he was revealed to be misleading them over his Stanford position. While Hogue was at the camp, a bike builder lost $20,000 worth of equipment and bike parts in a robbery. Hogue had stayed at the bike builder's home during his stay and was questioned by the police, but no further action was taken.

The following year, Hogue was working as a bicycle mechanic in St George, Utah, when a customer noticed he was using a tool engraved with the name of the bike builder in Colorado. He was charged, found guilty and given a one-to-five-year sentence, being released on parole after 10 months, in March 1989.

He missed a meeting with his parole officers in August that year because he was studying at Princeton – as Alexi Indris-Santana. Despite no high school qualifications, Indris-

Santana had been awarded a sponsorship and was admitted. Hogue claimed to be self-taught and that he had studied while working as a ranch hand in Utah. He said he hadn't slept indoors for a decade. His story – and falsified test scores – were enough to gain him admission.

Hogue deferred attending the university for a year due to his being incarcerated. (He told the university he was looking after his sick grandmother in Switzerland.) Once there, he did well academically, achieving As in most subjects. He also performed well athletically, but it was on the track that "Indris-Santana" came a cropper. At an Ivy League race meet in 1991, he was recognized by a student who had been at Palo Alto and was now at Yale. The student told the same reporter who had found him not to be Jay Huntsman. The officials at Princeton were alerted, and they annulled Santana's admission. The police were called in.

Hogue was given a nine-month jail sentence for wrongful impersonation and falsifying records. He also had to pay back the $22,000 track scholarship that Princeton had awarded him.

This wasn't the end of Hogue's criminal career. The day he was released from prison, he was immediately arrested for another crime. He had been given the job of cataloguing a collection of gemstones from Harvard's Mineralogical and Geological Museum. Fifty thousand dollars' worth of these gemstones were found in his room. He got 17 months for this theft.

In 1996, Hogue returned to Princeton but was thrown off campus for pretending to be a geology student called "Jim MacAuthor". He had been banned from the campus.

Although his days of conning those in the education world were over, his criminal behaviour wasn't. In 2007, Hogue was jailed for robbery. He'd stolen around seven thousand items, including artworks and sports goods worth $100,000, from properties in Telluride, Colorado, over a year-long period. For that, he spent four years behind bars.

He showed no sign of reform, being found guilty of squatting in 2017. He had been living in a camouflaged shack on the side of Aspen Mountain. When he was arrested, he was found to be in possession of stolen goods such as ski equipment, designer clothes, tools and construction materials, which he was selling online. He received a jail sentence of six years.

In 2021, the 61-year-old Hogue was arrested by police looking into a burglary and potential energy theft. A power cable was spotted being run from a house into his SUV.

During his trial for his Telluride crimes, Hogue wrote to the judge, "It's hard to explain why I do this. It's nothing I can really understand myself."

COMPLETELY NUTS

A quack has two meanings: the sound a duck makes, and someone who pretends they have medical skills. One of the latter types was John Romulus Brinkley, born in the Appalachian Mountains of North Carolina in the US in 1885.

Once out of school, he worked as a railway company telegrapher. Brinkley got married in 1907 to Sally Wike, and the two set out for a life on the road, selling fake medicines while pretending to be doctors.

The couple and their baby daughter began living in Chicago, where Brinkley enrolled at Bennett Medical College of Eclectic Medicine and Surgery, a for-profit school where academic standards and teaching practices were not high. He went back to working as a telegrapher, working nights to try to make ends meet, but his debts kept increasing.

In 1911, Brinkley left Chicago – and unpaid tuition fees – behind and moved to North Carolina to rejoin his wife, who had left him (not for the first time) and returned there. He started offering his services as an undergraduate physician, but nothing much came of it.

He resolved to rejuvenate his dreams of becoming a doctor and left for Missouri, where he bought a diploma from the

Eclectic Medical University in Kansas City. Not recognized by the Missouri State Board of Health, this "university" was a diploma mill – where qualifications were sold without any rigorous academic achievements necessary.

In 1913, Brinkley set up a business in Greenville, South Carolina, with a man calling himself Dr Burke (his real name was James Crawford). Brinkley and Crawford took their business inspiration from a Dr Burke, who had run a practice dealing with sexual diseases in Tennessee despite not having a medical qualification.

The two Greenville "Electro Medic Doctors" offered their services to men worried about their virility. For $25 a time, the men would receive an injection of coloured water. After a short period, the two "doctors" left town and unpaid bills behind. Brinkley's wife had also left him for the final time, permanently giving up on him and his desire to pursue a medical career.

After a move to Memphis, Brinkley became a bigamist, marrying Minnie Jones, the daughter of a local doctor. On his honeymoon, he was arrested for impersonating a doctor and not paying his bills in Greenville. His partner-in-crime Crawford paid the fines, and soon Brinkley was on his way again, this time to Arkansas.

There, he took over a doctor's office and made enough money to pay his outstanding fees from Bennett Medical College. Off again, Brinkley, Minnie and their son moved to Kansas City, where he re-enrolled at the Eclectic Medical University to finish the education he had started at Bennett. He graduated in 1915.

After a very brief period of service in the First World War (he was discharged after collapsing with exhaustion),

Brinkley began working as a doctor in Milford, Kansas. He treated patients during the Spanish Influenza pandemic but then hit on the idea that was to make his name and fortune.

An elderly patient came to see him regarding a problem he had with his virility. When Brinkley told him that when working at a meat-packing plant, he'd discovered that the goat was a healthy animal resistant to human diseases, the patient, who was a farmer, suggested that the solution would be to have a pair of goat testicles implanted next to his own. Brinkley, who was at first repulsed by the idea, changed his mind, and the procedure took place, the first one of many, at $150 a pop. The farmer was pleased with the results, and word spread.

Unsurprisingly, there was no scientific evidence behind the implants – which were also performed on women, placing goat ovaries near the human ones – and there were risks of infection. Brinkley was said to be often inebriated when operating, and sterilization was at a minimum. An unknown number of patients died.

When one of his patients gave birth to a boy, Brinkley seized on the opportunity and used it for advertising, claiming success for the "first goat-gland baby". It wasn't just reproduction that was offered – the operations were said to treat dementia and cancerous tumours.

With the increased public attention came scrutiny from the medical profession. One of those interested was Dr Morris Fishbein.

In 1922, Brinkley was invited by Harry Chandler, the owner of the *Los Angeles Times*, to perform one of his transplant operations on him. When the operation was a success,

Chandler gave the surgeon press exposure that brought him new clients, including movie stars.

It also brought him more investigation from Dr Fishbein, who testified against Brinkley and his unreliable CV at the Medical Board of California when he applied for a medical licence.

Looking for another outlet for marketing his services, Brinkley set up his own radio station in 1923. He combined medical advice with playing music and gospel services. Using the KFKB – "Kansas First, Kansas Best" – station, Brinkley started offering patients treatments available from pharmacies that formed part of the Brinkley Pharmaceutical Association. Listeners to the radio broadcasts were given numbers that identified certain prescriptions, which could be supplied only from pharmacies that were part of the association. They saw their income increase substantially as a result, as the price for the medicines was inflated, and the pharmacy kept some of the profit while the rest was Brinkley's. He was making around $14,000 a week from this line of business. These profits gave Brinkley the money to pay for improved infrastructure in Milford, as well as sponsoring a baseball team: the Brinkley Goats.

When diploma mills came under suspicion, indictments were issued for some "doctors" who had received their degrees from them. Brinkley was one of them, but the Kansas governor refused to extradite him to California as he was too profitable for the state.

When patients started reporting feeling unwell to their own doctors, the American Medical Association was called in but was unable to stop Brinkley. However, the Kansas Medical Board could, rescinding his medical licence in 1930, calling his actions "organized charlatanism".

Brinkley wasn't finished. He campaigned to become state governor so that he could appoint friendly members of the medical board who could reinstate his licence to practise medicine and print money. He stood three times but lost all of them.

When Brinkley's radio station was shut down after complaints it wasn't acting in the public's interest, he started broadcasting from over the border via a powerful radio transmitter in Mexico so powerful listeners in Canada could hear his broadcasts. The Mexican authorities were happy to assist Brinkley as it brought them revenue.

Based in Texas, Brinkley still performed transplant operations, among other procedures. Patients were given injections of "Formula 1020", which turned out to be coloured water. His vast earnings – thought to be in the region of a million dollars a year – through selling radio adverts and his own medical work gave him the money to live a luxurious life in a Texan mansion with a garage filled with Cadillacs.

Dr Fishbein had not given up. Now editor of the *Journal of the American Medical Association*, in 1938, he published an article entitled "Modern Medical Charlatans", where Brinkley's ethics and the medical effectiveness of his goat-testicle transplants were questioned. Brinkley sued the author for libel, claiming $250,000 in damages, but the damage was to be far more substantial: Brinkley lost, being called a charlatan and a quack.

Subsequent lawsuits for malpractice and investigations by the Internal Revenue Service cleaned him out. By 1941, he was bankrupt. The US Post Office pursued him on charges of using the mail to send out misleading advertisements, but he never faced them in court, dying in 1942 of heart failure. One of the claims sent out to potential customers was that Brinkley's treatments would enable them to live to be a hundred. Brinkley died aged 56.

LUSTIG FOR LIFE

To be a con artist, you need to have supreme belief in your abilities. You can't show any sign of vulnerability or fear. One man who showed the highest level of confidence in his confidence trickery was Victor Lustig, born in what is now the Czechia in 1890. He was to perform one of the most famous cons in history.

Lustig was in his teens when he began his criminal career, travelling around Europe. He started by pickpocketing and shoplifting but moved on to cons that saw him steal jewellery on the pretence of having it valued.

Despite spending several periods in prison, continuing with crime seemed to offer an easier way to receive other people's money than working for a living, and he moved on to working the trans-Atlantic liners. He was an expert card shark and was happy to relieve rich travellers of their money. One victim said, "He could make a deck of cards do everything but talk." The charming Lustig had a dignified and polite manner, acting as a gentleman. He adopted various aristocratic aliases: Earl Mountjoy or Baron von Kessler. He would eventually use an estimated 45 aliases, including that of Count Lustig.

When the First World War interrupted civilian liner services, Lustig stayed in the US, where he continued swindling money, at one point managing to take money for a repossessed property from a bank while also keeping the bonds he was issuing on the property. One of "Tricky Vic's" scams was to pretend to be a producer of a Broadway show, looking for investors.

In 1925, he returned to Europe when in Paris, hit on the scheme with which he would forever be associated: he would sell the Eiffel Tower. France's iconic landmark – the world's tallest building at the time – had been a feature of the Parisian skyline since 1889.

Lustig read in a newspaper article that the tower was in need of expensive repair, and there were suggestions that it might be pulled down. At the time of its construction, there had been complaints about its lack of aesthetic value.

With an accomplice called "Dapper" Don Collins, Lustig set about his plan. He used a forger to create authentic-looking government stationery, then sent out invitations to five businessmen in the scrap metal trade. They were invited to attend a presentation to be held in a Paris hotel.

After they'd arrived, Lustig appeared in the guise of the Deputy Director-General of the Ministry for Post and Telegraphs. He told them that the tower was too expensive to maintain and that it was to be demolished.

The iron would be a lucrative resource to acquire, and the scrap metal merchants were invited to submit their bids. Its 330-metre-high structure was an attractive opportunity, being composed of over 7,000 tonnes of wrought iron.

André Poisson, being new to Paris and keen to make his mark, looked the most likely to fall for their ruse, so Lustig met with him privately. Lustig told the ambitious Poisson that despite being a deputy director-general, he was on a very low salary considering the responsibility of his job. Poisson took the bait. A bunch of francs appeared, and Lustig gratefully took his bribe. Poisson wrote out a cheque for the initial payment as the successful bidder, and soon Lustig was on his way to Austria, after having banked the money.

Once in Austria he kept an eye on the newspapers to see if Poisson had gone to the police, but after a suitable period, he was sure they had not been alerted. He went back to Paris to repeat the scam. It didn't quite work out as before after one of the recipients of an invitation alerted the police. Lustig found out he was under suspicion and was soon heading over the Atlantic on a liner.

Lustig had other means of swindling money from vulnerable marks. One was the "Rumanian" or "Money" Box. It was a small wooden box which promised to duplicate any form of paper currency. In reality, Lustig placed genuine notes inside the box, ready to be produced when "copied" by the device. He sold his money-making boxes for upwards of $10,000; one went for $100,000 to a banker in Los Angeles.

Customers included an Oklahoman sheriff, who had arrested Lustig. One night in the cells, the persuasive conman was able to sell one of these boxes to the law official, who allowed Lustig to escape. When he found he had been conned, the sheriff pursued Lustig to Chicago, where the fraudster convinced the lawman he was using the machine wrongly.

He gave him his money back – in the form of counterfeit notes. When the sheriff used them in New Orleans, he was arrested and jailed for distributing counterfeit money.

Audacious to the core, Lustig even conned notorious Mafia boss Al Capone. Lustig convinced Capone he was honest by borrowing $50,000 from the gangster to invest in a get-rich-quick scheme, then returned all the money when the scheme fell through. Or at least, that's what he told the gangster. Lustig had no intention of investing the money and only took it in order to return it, as a way to build trust. When Lustig then asked Capone for a much smaller amount of money, $5,000, he was given it. He kept this.

In 1935, Lustig went into the banknote counterfeiting business. For the next five years, an estimated $2.3 million dollars, of "Lustig money" entered circulation. It ended when Lustig's mistress, Billie Mae Scheible, reported him to the police after she suspected he was fooling around with another woman. Lustig was arrested – something he was used to, having been apprehended 40 times in his life of crime. In his possession he had a locker key. The locker contained the plates for printing the fake notes and over $50,000 in cash. The year following Lustig's arrest, the number of counterfeit notes seized in the US dropped by half.

Never one to admit defeat, Lustig escaped from a federal detention centre in New York by clambering down a rope, wiping at the windows as if a window cleaner. When federal agents apprehended him a month later in Pittsburgh, Lustig said, "Well, boys, here I am." At his trial, he was given 15 years for the counterfeiting and an extra five for the escape. He was sent to the notorious prison, Alcatraz.

In December 1947, Lustig became ill when still in prison and died a few days later. His death certificate (which had his name as "Robert Miller", one of Lustig's pseudonyms) recorded his occupation as "apprentice salesman and counterfeiter".

PRUSSIAN ABOUT

Occasionally, newspapers will run stories of those caught out dressing up as soldiers. They might have attended a remembrance parade wearing a military beret, blazer and assorted regimental badges or medals. They are found out when those in the know see a discrepancy, perhaps a medal for service in a conflict the wearer was too young to have taken part in. These figures are lambasted and can face criminal charges.

One military impersonator, however, who received something very different was Wilhelm Voigt, known as the Captain of Köpenick. Born in 1849, Voigt was a cobbler by trade but also a habitual criminal, who by the age of 57 had spent half his life in prison on theft or forgery charges.

He was released in February 1906 after a 15-year jail term. Determined to live a crime-free life, he was thwarted by bureaucratic inability to provide him with a passport. Without this document, he could be thrown out of any town and would find it difficult to find work. A shoemaker in the northern German city of Wismar took Voigt in, offering him work. He was a good worker, but when his lack of official papers saw him lose his job, it was a turning point.

On 16 October 1906, Voigt pulled on the uniform of a Prussian officer. A uniform he had bought second-hand.

He had the grey greatcoat, blue and red cap, white gloves and sword. Gaining a criminal conviction for theft when a boy had meant he would not be permitted to join the military as he'd wanted. Now, he would remedy that.

At an army barracks, he ordered a small group of real soldiers to accompany him to the town of Köpenick, a few miles outside of Berlin. They automatically assumed he was a bona fide officer, and so fell into line. When he encountered a second group at a shooting range, he had them follow him, too. They all got on a train, the captain in second class, his men in third.

Once in Köpenick, Voigt marched them to the town hall. He ordered the mayor to be arrested, as there were discrepancies with the civic bookkeeping. The town clerk was also detained. The fake officer confiscated 4,000 marks and left his troops behind to guard the town hall, allowing no one in or out. Voigt disappeared with the money.

A manhunt began with 2,500 marks offered as a reward for the thieving officer's arrest. Ten days later, Voigt was in custody. At his trial, he was found guilty on charges of unauthorized wearing of uniform, unlawful detention of others, theft and forgery (for writing a false name on the receipt he gave for the money). He was given a four-year prison sentence.

In Germany, the public regarded Voigt as a folk hero. There was great amusement that such a thing could happen in a country where the military was held in high regard. The fact that a shambling, sunken-cheeked man in his 50s could be taken to be a Prussian officer was hilarious to many.

Plays and books were quickly written to cash in on the case. Postcards featuring Voigt in uniform were printed off in their thousands. Many were sent to the town hall in Köpenick.

Voigt only served two years of his sentence as a very important person gave him a pardon: the Kaiser, Wilhelm II. The commander of Germany's armed forces was said to have been amused by the incident, calling him an "amiable rogue".

Out of prison, Voigt enjoyed being a celebrity, selling autographs and making public appearances both in Europe and North America. Madame Tussauds ensured his fame by putting a Captain Köpenick wax figure on display. A more permanent representation was made in 1996 when a bronze statue of Voigt as the captain was placed at the Köpenick town hall steps – immortalized forever as the soldier he became.

ROGER, OVER AND OUT

Roger Charles Doughty-Tichborne was born in 1829, the eldest son of wealthy parents James, the 10th Baronet of Tichborne, and Henriette Tichborne. They owned large tracts of land in Hampshire, England.

Roger fell in love with his first cousin, Katherine Doughty, but her father was against any marriage. He laid a condition that if they were still in love after three years, then he would allow them to wed.

Roger went abroad to see the world and forget about the situation. He travelled around South America before, in 1854, boarding a ship sailing to New York. The ship never made it, going down in a storm; all on board were lost. Roger's father was heartbroken by the loss and died in 1862.

Roger was officially declared dead in 1857. Despite this, his mother refused to believe her son was gone, her belief backed by a clairvoyant. She began a search, placing notices in newspapers in Australia and South America, stating that a "handsome reward" would be paid for information on her son's whereabouts. He was described as "of a delicate constitution, rather tall with very light brown hair and blue eyes". It was thought that some survivors from the sunken ship might have been taken to Australia.

In 1865, an illiterate butcher called Arthur Orton, living in Wagga Wagga in Australia, heard about the case. Orton had fled England to evade creditors and, in Australia, was going under the name "Thomas Castro". (Orton had previously spent time in South America when employed as a sailor, something that would have an effect on his case.) He was unable to fully read the newspaper but had it explained to him. He decided to act.

He told a lawyer called William Gibbes that he was the missing baronet. As evidence, he produced a pipe with the initials "RCT" engraved on it. This was proof enough for Gibbes, who wrote to the real Roger's mother with the news her son had been found. She was overjoyed and urged him to come home.

Orton first went to Sydney, where his claim passed the first hurdle when he was interviewed by Francis Turville, the governor's private secretary. Turville thought because he didn't appear to be putting any effort into convincing anyone he was an English aristocrat that he must be one. He did think him a bit dirty, and his English wasn't that polished.

The second hurdle was meeting a Tichborne family servant, who let Henriette know that this man was her missing son. The way was clear for Orton to sail to England.

While some thought he was Roger, others did not and saw through him immediately. A village blacksmith living near to the family home said, "If you are Sir Roger, you've changed from a racehorse to a carthorse."

Orton weighed 280 pounds, much more than the slim gentleman who'd left a decade before. Orton had dark and wavy hair. He was too old, too uncouth, couldn't speak French, and crucially didn't have a tattoo on his arm, unlike the missing heir.

There was one person to whom the veracity of Orton's claims meant the most: Henriette. The two met in Paris, and despite suspicious requests from Orton, such as wanting the room to be kept unlit and covering his face with a handkerchief, she took the man in front of her to be her son. Henriette granted him a thousand pounds annual allowance, but he wanted more. Orton went to England to stake his claim for the family estate and title.

Vincent Gosford was a friend of the real Roger and had been given a copy of a letter Roger wrote to his intended wife before departing England. When Gosford mentioned the letter to the imposter, Orton was completely ignorant of it. He also failed to recognize his long-lost love, Katherine.

Determined to produce sufficient evidence, the "Tichborne Claimant" travelled to South America to prove that, as Roger, he'd been to certain places. The plan backfired as those he spoke to didn't know of any Roger Tichborne but did recall an "Arthur Orton". Castro explained this away by saying that he had known Orton when they were cattle ranchers together, and they sometimes exchanged names to avoid detection after some possibly criminal activity carried out together.

In May 1871, a legal hearing began to determine Orton's claim. His case fell apart on a number of points: as well as the missing tattoo, there were questions about why he could no longer play chess or read music.

At one point, he made the shocking assertion that before he left England, Katherine and he were lovers. She vehemently denied such a slur on her character.

The 103-day hearing ended with Orton not getting the keys to the manor house. He was, beyond doubt, an imposter. Instead, after another marathon trial (lasting 188 days due to 450 witnesses being called), he was locked up for 14 years for perjury. In his sentencing remarks, Mr Justice Mellor said about Orton's aspersions on Katherine's character, "No more foul or deliberate falsehood was ever heard in a court of justice."

These trials caught the imagination of the public, with a split among the population emerging: the working class hoped for a win for Orton, and while the upper class wished to see him defeated.

When released in 1884, Orton sold his story to a newspaper and admitted he wasn't Sir Roger Tichborne. However, he went back on this and insisted he was the once-missing aristocrat. When he died in 1898, he was buried in a coffin with a card bearing Sir Roger's full name.

FORGERY

Forgery as an activity has been around for a long time. Art forgeries go back to at least as far as the Renaissance period. Michelangelo could turn his supremely talented hand to making copies of drawings by old masters and could chisel out reliefs by Donatello. Some were done as pranks, but others were sold as genuine antiques. A statue of Cupid was aged artificially and sold to a cardinal for 200 ducats. When the cleric found it was a fake, he demanded his money back.

The incident didn't hurt Michelangelo's career – if anything, it helped establish his reputation as a fine artist, something that was to happen to others in the future. Creating authentic-looking forgeries requires as much craftsmanship as creating an original.

In 1506, Albrecht Dürer tried to stop several engravers in both Germany and Italy from copying his prints, but he was unable to secure legal protection. It would take years until artists could gain copyright protection, but this wouldn't halt the illegal copier.

In 1896, the Louvre in Paris paid 200,000 French francs for an inscribed golden helmet from the third century BCE that was actually a nineteenth-century forgery by a Russian goldsmith.

Not all those who created artefacts in the style of older pieces did them to make money – some had other motives. Both would be able to fool the experts...

POETIC LICENCE

Thomas Chatterton was born in 1752, several months after his father, a Bristol schoolmaster, had died. Aged eight, Chatterton was sent to a charity school and then employed as a scribe by a local lawyer. Copying legal documents was torment for the young boy, who wanted to write poetry. When Chatterton's employer found out about his creative outlet, he beat him and forbade him from continuing.

It was in vain.

Chatterton had family connections to a parish church in Bristol dating back to the twelfth century. For more than 150 years, his father's family had been sextons at St Mary Redcliffe Church, which was regarded as one of the finest Gothic churches in England. Queen Elizabeth I called it "the fairest, goodliest and most famous parish church in England".

The young Chatterton took inspiration from the church. He was fascinated by the altar tombs of notable figures from Bristol's past, such as William II Canynges, the merchant turned priest of the fifteenth century, and the thirteenth-century knight Robert de Berkeley. He also found old parchment documents inside a chest in the church.

As a young child (before he went to the charity school), Chatterton had used the Bible to learn to read, so he was used to old styles of writing. He read as much as he could and became acquainted with the works of Chaucer and Edmund Spenser. He drew inspiration from them into his own writing. Using parchment that he had made look suitably aged by rubbing it on the ground, Chatterton began writing poems in the Medieval style, as if from the pen of Thomas Rowley, a fifteenth-century monk he had invented. Chatterton sent some of "Rowley's" poems to several notable figures in Bristol to attract attention and forge useful connections. It wasn't just poetical works Chatterton could produce. He provided forged maps, property deeds, lists of ancient monuments and Medieval histories of Bristol's churches. He created a fake family tree dating back to William the Conqueror for one such man, Henry Burgum, who was pleased to see he was descended from nobility. For this service, Burgum paid Chatterton five shillings. However, when Burgum sent the family lineage to be verified by the official heraldic authority, the College of Arms, they responded by telling him it was completely false. He was humiliated and subjected to scorn. His fortunes declined, and he was eventually declared bankrupt.

Chatterton expended great effort on his forgeries, working late and keeping a glossary of supposedly ancient terms in a notebook. He composed a 1,400-line long dramatic poem but failed to get it published. He sent a sample to an antiquarian publisher called James Dodsley and suggested he might provide a guinea for his trouble in copying the sample from the original, but this was declined.

Failing to gain a sufficient income, Chatterton tried the well-known writer, historian and politician Horace Walpole, the son of Robert Walpole, the first prime minister of Britain.

Walpole initially showed interest but, after consulting with some poets he knew, rejected "Rowley's" work, believing them to be inauthentic. Chatterton's hopes of patronage from Walpole were gone.

Chatterton changed tack and found success with non-poetical writing, his work appearing in several periodicals, including *Town and Country Magazine*. He wrote satirical and political pieces targeting the great and the good of the time, including former prime ministers and the Princess of Wales.

In the spring of 1770, he moved to London to capitalize on his writing talents. His success continued but a crackdown by the government on satirical works (seen as anti-government) meant this line of employment dried up. After this, Chatterton's writing did not provide enough money – he was unable to afford food – and when his rent was increased, his spirits waned. He did write one further Thomas Rowley work, an *Excelente Balade of Charitie*, which was rejected by the magazine he submitted it to. It includes these lines:

Liste! now the thunder's rattling clymmynge sound
Cheves slowlie on, and then embollen clangs,
Shakes the hie spyre, and losst, dispended, drown'd,
Still on the gallard eare of terroure hanges.

Before he left Bristol earlier that year, Chatterton had freed himself from his employer's contract by threatening suicide. On 24 August, he died by his own hand, after swallowing opium then arsenic. There are differing views on whether he died deliberately, seeing nothing but failure ahead of him, or if it was accidental, the arsenic being a treatment at the time for a sexually transmitted disease. (Chatterton consorted with prostitutes.) Whatever lay behind his death, he was only 17 years old.

After death, Chatterton became well-regarded for his writing talents by some of the most famous writers of the Romantic period, such as Browning, Coleridge and Shelley. Keats called him "the purest writer in the English language", and William Wordsworth described him as "the marvellous boy, The sleepless soul that perished in his pride".

The fame and reputation that Chatterton had yearned for had arrived too late.

FAKE VIEWS

There is a fascination with knowing what historical figures were really thinking as they carried out their grand plans. Memoirs and interviews can give us some insight, but these are often written with hindsight, allowing the writer time to deliver the best view of themselves.

A quote attributed to Winston Churchill says, "History will be kind to me, for I intend to write it." And this he did in his six-volume history of the Second World War. But what about his chief enemy during that conflict, Adolf Hitler?

Given his suicide in 1945, there was no opportunity to find out the Führer's thoughts.

That is, until 1983, four decades after his death. In April of that year, German magazine *Stern* announced to a stunned world that they were in possession of diaries that belonged to Hitler and that they were going to publish them. British newspaper *The Sunday Times* also wished to serialize the contents. The paper's owner, Rupert Murdoch, jetted in to secure the rights during the bidding war.

There were 60 volumes of the Hitler diaries. It cost *Stern* 9.3 million Deutsche Marks to acquire this valuable newly-found insight into the thinking of one of the twentieth century's key historical figures.

Where had these journals come from after all that time? The story went that the diaries were in an aircraft carrying Hitler's personal possessions, which crashed near Dresden near the end of the war in 1945. The notebooks were then kept by an East German official.

The journals came to *Stern* via one of its journalists, Gerd Heidemann, who had a keen interest in Germany's Nazi past (he had acquired a yacht belonging to the former senior Nazi Hermann Göring and even took things to a more personal level by having an affair with Göring's daughter, Edda). The purchase of the ex-Nazi's yacht had put Heidemann into financial difficulties, and he was keen to secure new income.

The diaries contained trivial nuggets such as Hitler complaining of flatulence and girlfriend Eva Braun telling her future husband he had bad breath. The leader of the Third Reich had also been irritated by Braun's wish to get free tickets to the 1936 Berlin Olympics.

On a far more serious level, the Führer expressed concern for the well-being of Germany's Jewish population, something that might raise eyebrows to anyone with even the scantest knowledge of twentieth-century European history. He praised Soviet Union leader Joseph Stalin for his harsh treatment of his officers.

It was good for business – *Stern*'s special edition featuring excerpts (which was sold at an increased price from the regular edition) sold over 2.2 million copies, up 400,000 from its normal circulation figure.

The diaries seemed too good to be true, and that's because they were. A German forger called Konrad Kujau had written every word.

Kujau had a history of faking luncheon vouchers before moving on to Nazi memorabilia such as poems and an introduction to the third volume of *Mein Kampf* (there were only two real volumes), which he sold from his shop in Stuttgart. He had made paintings supposedly by the hand of Adolf Hitler, including a nude study of Eva Braun.

Within just a few weeks, the diaries were declared to be forgeries. A headline in Rupert Murdoch's *New York Post* said it succinctly: "Hitler's Diaries are Fake".

When *Stern* had first received the notebooks in May 1981, they had not noticed a glaring clue that the diaries were not authentic. Each book cover was labelled "FH" rather than the supposed writer's initials, "AH" – the forger had confused the Gothic letter F for A. Further evidence of their fakery: the paper used did not exist in the 1930s. It was first used in the 1950s.

Details in the diaries had been verified by German experts, unfortunately using the same sourcebook as the one the forger had used. One expert had also been supplied handwriting samples of Hitler's and, unsurprisingly, they matched.

The reputations of *Stern*'s editors were trashed. The journalist Heidemann and the forger Kujau were found guilty of fraud and given four-year jail terms. British historian Hugh Trevor-Roper, who had initially stated they were the real thing and that they could change the way the history of the period was written, quickly expressed doubts as to their veracity. He admitted his error, but the damage to his reputation was done.

Rupert Murdoch said in 2012, "It was a massive mistake I made, and I will have to live with it for the rest of my life."

ARTFUL DODGERS

Genuine artworks by great artists such as van Gogh, Picasso or Monet can command high prices, in the tens of millions of dollars. Crucial to their price is the provenance – the documentation that proves their history and certainty of being created by the relevant artist. When this paperwork is forged – and the artwork is convincing enough to look genuine – then there is great potential for fraud.

When he was younger, John Myatt had wanted to make his living from painting and had gone to art college. In the 1970s, he was working as a songwriter in the music industry. (He claimed to have written a number one hit single called "Silly Games", but his attribution is disputed.) During this time, Myatt painted a couple of pictures in the style of French Fauvist artist Raoul Dufy as an executive he knew was thinking of buying a real one. Instead, the executive hung them on his wall, where they were admired and accepted as genuine.

After leaving London for rural Staffordshire, Myatt started teaching art at schools and colleges. In 1985, Myatt had to give up teaching after his marriage break-up left him with two children to care for. Myatt needed income from a job he could do while still at home. He offered his painting impersonation skills in return for payment and placed an advert in the British satirical magazine *Private Eye*, offering "19th and 20th century fakes for £150".

Commissions came from clients mostly wanting Impressionist works. Myatt avoided doing pre-Raphaelite paintings as they took too long, being so detailed. One client wanted a picture in the style of Joshua Reynolds that depicted a Royal Navy admiral staring out to sea, but with the client's own face so that he could claim ancestry to this notable maritime figure.

Myatt wasn't attempting to hoodwink anyone at this stage. What was a legitimate business turned criminal, however, since the works he created were so convincing, they were sold as genuine through Sotheby's and Christie's auction houses.

The man behind these sales was John Drewe, who had recognized the potential of making serious money through Myatt's talents. Drewe had ordered a Matisse from him and went on to commission a dozen more. In 1987, Myatt painted a work in the style of French Cubist artist Albert Gleizes. Drewe took it to an auction house, without informing Myatt, where it was valued at £25,000. This started the run of forgeries from Myatt's easel. While the money was welcome, he was also flattered by the attention his works were receiving. He felt important.

Myatt went on to paint around 180 fake works by twentieth-century artists such as Marc Chagall, Alberto Giacometti and Henri Matisse. Myatt used domestic emulsion paints as they were cheaper than the traditional oil paint and thought no one would be fooled by his not using the proper materials.

Through charm and financial donations, Drewe was able to gain access to the archives of major art galleries such as the Tate. Once in, he placed faked certificates of authenticity and photographs of Myatt's forged works into the gallery's records. Having this "proof" ensured they would be taken as authentic and so would be worth more.

However, the run was about to end. In 1995, Myatt and Drewe were arrested. Drewe's ex-wife had found incriminating documents in his flat. Myatt pleaded guilty to conspiracy to defraud and was given a sentence of one year in jail.

After a lengthy trial where he defended himself, Drewe was sentenced to six years in prison for conspiracy to defraud, forgery, theft and false accounting. He was sent to the notorious Victorian jail, Pentonville Prison.

London's Metropolitan police force called it "the biggest contemporary art fraud of the twentieth century". Police estimated Drewe to have earned at least £2.5 million from the sales of the forgeries. Around 60 paintings by Myatt are thought to have been recovered, with the rest still in circulation.

When in prison, Myatt used his talents to draw portraits of his fellow inmates in exchange for phone cards which were used to call family and friends. After serving four months, the artful forger was released.

He has since presented several television shows where his talents of artistic impersonation are shown. He has continued to paint "genuine fakes" for sale, where they are clearly labelled "in the style of". Whether the fake connoisseur is after a van Gogh *The Starry Night*, a David Hockney *The Splash* or a *Mona Lisa* by Leonardo da Vinci, they can all be ordered. A Monet *Water Lilies* picture can be had for just £35,000. In 2018, an actual Monet *Water Lilies* painting fetched $84.6 million at auction in New York.

JOYCE TO THE WORLD

When Joyce Hatto died in June 2006, aged 77, the music world mourned her passing. *The Guardian* newspaper described her as "one of the greatest pianists Britain has ever produced". She had died after suffering from ovarian cancer since the early 1990s, although some reports stated she had been diagnosed in the early 1970s and that this had hastened her retirement from playing live in 1976.

Hatto had begun playing in the 1940s and had a successful career performing major works in the UK and around Europe, sometimes with the London Symphony Orchestra. She supplemented her performing income by working as a piano teacher. One of her pupils was the future novelist Rose Tremain.

In 1956, Hatto married William Barrington-Coupe, the A&R manager for a record company. He became her manager. Barrington-Coupe attempted to import radios from Hong Kong without paying purchase tax and was found guilty of tax avoidance in 1966. He was sent to jail for a year and fined £3,600.

After retiring, Hatto lived out of the public eye until the early 2000s, when recordings of her piano recitals were released on the Concert Artists label, which was owned by her husband.

Over one hundred recordings included her performances of the greats of classical music: Beethoven, Brahms, Chopin, Liszt, Mozart and Schubert. She also recorded Leopold Godowsky's 54 *Studies on Chopin's Études*, commonly accepted as the most difficult piano music ever composed.

The recordings brought her name widespread attention in the classical music world. Her work was given positive reviews, with one describing Hatto as "the greatest living pianist that almost no one has ever heard of". Music lovers were keen to hear this music. There were doubts by some fans, who wondered how an ill and elderly woman was able to play so much great music.

However, in 2007 – the year after Hatto died – one listener noticed something strange. When listening to a CD of Hatto playing the *Transcendental Études* by Liszt, his computer displayed the name of another musician: László Simon. The music database linked to the audio files was displaying the correct musician's name. The listener contacted a music critic who had praised Hatto's recordings.

When the critic listened to Hatto's playing, his suspicions grew. A classical music magazine then gave Hatto's recordings to a musical expert, who found that it wasn't Hatto playing – it was a range of other pianists. Ninety-two of them, to be exact. Hatto's husband had simply taken recordings by other musicians and released them as if they were by his wife. Some of the original recordings were slowed down to disguise their origins. Godowsky's 54 studies were, in fact, performed by the Italian pianist Carlo Grante.

When the scandal broke, Barrington-Coupe insisted the music was by his late wife. He later said that he had only inserted sections by other musicians to cover any weaknesses in his wife's playing or yells of pain caused by her illness. He had done it to provide recognition for his wife's talents, which he thought had been overlooked, and not for the money.

Sales were in the low thousands, and he had actually lost money, although one online music retailer was said to have done £50,000 of business with Barrington-Coupe. Joyce Hatto was said to be unaware of the forgeries. No charges were brought, and Barrington-Coupe died in 2014.

The editor of *Gramophone* magazine wrote, "the classical music world has never known a scandal like this".

ART ATTACK

The master in the dark arts of art forgery was Tom Keating, born in Lewisham in London in 1917. Keating admitted having painted over 2,000 fake paintings by over a hundred artists in 25 years. What made Keating different from most others talented in the ways of reproducing the styles of the great painters is that he wasn't in it to profit financially.

He left school aged 14 and started painting houses – not artistically, but in his father's house painting business. Keating did art at evening classes, but war interrupted, and he served in the Royal Navy.

Keating gained entry to Goldsmiths' College but failed, being told his paintings lacked originality in composition. He then found work as a painting restorer. It was while doing this that he painted his first "Sexton Blake" – rhyming slang for "fake". He had been challenged by Fred Roberts, the owner of the restoring business he was working for, to create a painting as good as that by twentieth-century British artist Frank Moss Bennett. Keating's own work was then sold by Roberts, with Moss's signature magically appearing in place of the actual creator's.

This event sparked something inside Keating. He felt aggrieved at the art world, where profits were made by dealers and yet the artists themselves were struggling to survive. He resolved to show them up: he would flood the market with paintings. This would lower the price and so reduce the dealer's profits. He would make them easily identifiable as not being genuine.

Keating personalized some of the works in unique ways: in lead white paint he would add a signature, a rude word or the simple word "fake". If these works were subjected to X-rays, these additions would be clearly visible. He would sometimes add small figures, such as the original artist or even himself. In his version of the famous *Fighting Temeraire* by J. M. W. Turner, he inserted the figure of an artist being arrested.

Keating could create works in the styles of Constable, Degas, Renoir, Rembrandt and Rubens, but it was another artist that was to be crucial to his story. In 1963, Keating began creating works inspired by nineteenth-century British landscape watercolourist Samuel Palmer.

In 1976, it was these "Palmer" works that brought Keating notoriety. His artworks came under suspicion and were found to be on modern paper. He was charged with criminal deception and appeared in court.

Jane Kelly, who had previously been in a relationship with Keating, admitted obtaining money through the sale of the fakes and was given a suspended jail sentence. She gave evidence against Keating, but the trial was abandoned due to his ill health. The stress of the trial, his years of smoking and breathing in noxious fumes while restoring paintings, had taken their effect on his heart.

After the trial and the associated publicity, Keating and his paintings increased in value. An auction of his artworks sold for over half a million pounds. He was offered a contract with a London art gallery worth £250,000. He appeared on television as the presenter of a show where he showed how to paint in the style of great artists such as van Gogh and Turner.

Keating affirmed that if he could afford to, he'd give all his paintings away for free. He once said, "I believe the ability to paint is a gift from God. If you've got this ability, then it should be used to bring pleasure." Tom Keating died in 1984, aged 66.

SHAKESPEARE'S SWINDLER

William Shakespeare is still regarded as the greatest writer of the English language, centuries after his death in 1616. His plays and sonnets are regularly performed around the world, with hundreds of words and quotations forming part of everyday speech.

While his canon of work is now well established, there was a time when it seemed like new works had been found. That time was the eighteenth century.

William Ireland – also known as Samuel, after his father – was born in 1777. He was his parents' third child and struggled to gain his father's approval or attention. Ireland's father was so disappointed with his son he questioned if he was really his offspring.

His father was a book publisher and collector of Shakespeare plays and relics. William Ireland accompanied his father on a visit to Stratford-upon-Avon, where his father bought several relics of the Bard, such as Shakespeare's "courting chair" and a purse given by the great writer to his wife, Anne Hathaway. They may not have been genuine, but his father's delight in their purchase certainly was.

Ireland was aware of Thomas Chatterton's poetical frauds several decades before and figured he could do the same.

He acquired some Elizabethan-era books and then removed blank pages, which he used to practise writing in the style of two centuries previously. He created the same type of ink used then and found techniques to help age the document, which included heating the paper.

He gave one of the books to his father, carefully inscribing it with a dedication from the author to the queen of the period, "Good Queen Bess" – Elizabeth I. Ireland's father was highly pleased with his present. Ireland followed this with a terracotta relief of Oliver Cromwell – also inscribed by a contemporary figure.

Ireland then proceeded to create letters and papers associated with Shakespeare. Papers featuring the Bard's own handwriting were a scarcity at the time (and still are), and there was great interest in the possibility of discovering more. Ireland's father had once said he would exchange half of his library for an example of Shakespeare's signature. Ireland worked on providing this. He produced items such as mortgage deeds; letters to (and from) Shakespeare's patron, the Earl of Southampton; a letter from Elizabeth I to Shakespeare; love letters to Anne Hathaway, Shakespeare's wife (with attached lock of hair); and a promissory note to the actor, John Heminge. An early version of *King Lear* was also "found".

Ireland's father was overjoyed and wanted to know where his son had managed to find these treasures. Ireland had concocted a backstory about an elderly gentleman he'd met in a coffee house, who was the owner of a stash of the Shakespeare papers. He did not divulge this man's full name but referred to him only as "Mr H".

An issue arose when a real signature of John Heminge was discovered that looked nothing like the one Samuel Ireland had. His son came up with a reason: there were two John Heminges who were actors. When a letter from the Earl of Leicester was suspected of being a forgery due to its being dated after the nobleman had died, Samuel Ireland just tore off that part of the document.

Samuel Ireland's collection grew and grew as his fame increased. Visitors were delighted to see these documents from Shakespeare. James Boswell, biographer of esteemed writer Samuel Johnson, fell to his knees and said he would die a happy man. Which he did a few months later.

The priceless relics of England's great playwright continued to appear: drawings, letters – even a lock of the great man's hair. But more was to come. What if there was an unseen play among the newly discovered documents?

Vortigern and Rowena was to be that play.

Taking inspiration from *Holinshed's Chronicles* – the history book Shakespeare himself had used – Ireland created a work based on the Anglo-Saxon king Vortigern and his mistress Rowena. He wrote the work in his own hand, saying Mr H wanted to retain the original but was happy to see him copy it out. The Drury Lane Theatre agreed to put on the play, but the venue's manager had reservations about its quality.

Both Irelands were paid up front, although Samuel kept the lion's share of the £300 received from the theatre. The play's first night was 2 April 1796. The acclaimed Shakespearean actor John Kemble, playing Vortigern, wished it to be the previous day (April Fool's Day) as he wasn't sure about the play's genuineness. The audience seemed to enjoy the performance through the first two acts, but as the play neared its end, they enjoyed it even more – laughing at some of the ineptly written lines. The humour continued during one of the actor's death throes when a curtain fell on him.

The unintendedly humorous production ended with the lines:

Thou clapp'st thy rattling fingers to thy sides,
And when this solemn mockery is o'er.

The play was not performed again. When it was announced to the audience that it would not be run again, those who thought it genuine started fighting with those who believed it a forgery.

The Irelands had made some money from the receipts; however, the reviews suggested the play was not a genuine Shakespearian piece but written by someone wishing to fool the public. Shakespeare expert Edmond Malone had published a book a month before laying out Ireland's work as being forgeries, noting the wrong use of language, chronology and style.

Samuel Ireland was suspected of being behind it, but he was blameless. His reputation was hugely damaged. William Ireland, who had done all the forgery, confessed, but his father refused to believe his son was capable of pulling off such a feat. Even when his son published notices in the newspapers admitting his culpability, his father still didn't accept it. The two become estranged, a situation that was still in place when Samuel died in 1800.

William Ireland went on to have a writing career, but it never gained anything like the attention or income of his days as Shakespeare. He wrote as himself but could, on occasion rattle off a "Shakespeare" text for a small fee. He never faced charges for the forgeries but did spend time in prison in York for debt. He died in 1835.

DE-LAUREY LOADS OF CASH

Joyti De-Laurey began working as a temp at investment bank Goldman Sachs in 1998. With husband Tony, she tried running a sandwich bar, but the business failed. She proved to be an efficient and competent secretary at the bank and was made a full-time PA (personal assistant) to Jennifer Moses, a managing director.

In the post, De-Laurey organized trips and meetings, and not just for her boss. She also assisted Moses's husband, Ron Beller, a partner at the firm. PAs were expected to go beyond the day-to-day functions required for their boss and take on extra tasks for their private lives. De-Laurey organized Moses's fortieth birthday celebrations in Rome.

As part of the job, De-Laurey was told by co-workers that she could sign cheques for her boss's private business, such as paying bills. With executives often travelling abroad, this would be the only way of settling payments. One day, De-Laurey had the notion to try writing a cheque to herself for £4,000 and signing her boss's name. No one noticed – so she kept doing it.

She went on to take £1.1 million from Moses and Beller. Money went on cars, jewellery and designer clothes from Louis Vuitton and Chanel. Expensive holidays were had abroad, including a first-class trip to see Lennox Lewis box Mike Tyson in the US. She also gave money to friends, family and charities.

De-Laurey's annual salary was £38,000, but no one at the company seemed to notice her new expensive jewellery and clothes. She told her family she was working in mergers and acquisitions, thus earning a high salary.

When Moses left the company in 2001, De-Laurey began working for Goldman Sachs partner Scott Mead. She took money from him too, forging his signature on transfer authorizations from his investment account to move large amounts to accounts she'd set up in Cyprus. One transfer was for £2.25 million.

In 2002, she was aiming to quit the bank and move to Cyprus with her husband Tony and their child. She had bought a villa for the family and had ordered a £150,000 speedboat for Tony. An Aston Martin V12 Vanquish worth £175,000 was also on its way.

However, her best-laid plans were about to come undone. Mead was going to give a six-figure donation to his alma mater, Harvard University. He asked De-Laurey for a statement, but she didn't produce it. Mead then contacted the bank, and when they told him of the transfers to the Bank of Cyprus, he realized he had been scammed. The police were called. Investigations found that De-Laurey had stolen £3.3 million from him.

Going to court, De-Laurey would be warmly greeted by passengers on the London Underground who felt she was a Robin Hood-type figure, getting one over on those earning astronomical sums at the big banks. She said she had received over 700 letters of support.

In her 16-week-long trial in 2004, De-Laurey claimed she was permitted to take money for her indispensable services – including covering up an affair – but this was strongly denied by the victims.

The judge called De-Laurey "duplicitous, deceitful and thoroughly dishonest". She had gained sympathy from her employers by claiming she had terminal cancer despite her having no such illness. She was convicted on 20 counts of fraud: 16 for obtaining a money transfer by deception and four for forgery, resulting in a sentence of seven years behind bars. She served three and a half. Her husband and mother – a general practice doctor called Devi Schahhou – were also convicted on money laundering charges. Schahhou had benefitted from her daughter's crimes by having her house's mortgage paid off and buying a property in Cyprus. She was given a suspended prison sentence. Tony spent six months in prison. De-Laurey and Tony later divorced.

Dubbed the "Picasso of con artists" by Mead, De-Laurey admitted after she was released, "I've got an illness only diamonds can cure."

KEEPING IT IN THE FAMILY

On 16 November 2007, Shaun Greenhalgh was sentenced to prison for four years and eight months for creating art forgeries and then laundering the proceeds. He had pleaded guilty to the charges. He wasn't the only member of his family to appear in court.

His 84-year-old father, George, and 83-year-old mother, Olive, were also there. Both were given suspended sentences, with wheelchair-bound George being told he would have gone to jail if he had been younger. The two had admitted conspiring to defraud between 1989 and 2006.

Shaun was responsible for manufacturing a range of artworks and artefacts. His dad, George, made the sales, convincing auction houses and experts in the UK, US and Europe of the authenticity of the items. Olive would make telephone calls to prospective buyers, as her son was too shy. Shaun had left school with no qualifications and didn't attend art school. However, he had a talent: creating pieces that appeared to stem from a different era. When still at school, he sold miniature Victorian clay pipes with representations of people on them that he'd fired in the art department's kilns.

This was just the start and, over time from a shed at his parents' terraced council house in Bolton, Shaun turned his creative hand to a range of fakes, whether they be Roman artefacts, Henry Moore sculptures, paintings by the great Impressionists, pastels by L. S. Lowry or many others. He made hundreds of artworks and artefacts. Shaun's talents across a range of periods, styles and mediums led to him being described by a detective as "the most gifted and diverse art forger we've ever dealt with".

The pieces themselves were not enough to convince art experts, and the Greenhalghs were effective in producing evidence of provenance. A statue called *The Faun*, supposedly by Paul Gauguin, was sold for £20,700 in 1994 at Sotheby's. It was later exhibited at the Art Institute of Chicago. Olive claimed to have inherited it from a relative who knew Gauguin. She was able to produce evidence in the form of a convincing sales invoice.

Shaun could also create Egyptian artefacts, and his *Amarna Princess* was the most successful. The 52-cm-high alabaster statue of the daughter of Queen Nefertiti and Pharaoh Akhenaten was sold for £440,000 in 2003. The buyer was Bolton Museum, which exhibited the 3,300-year-old relic, which had been authenticated by Christie's and the British Museum. Tools from a DIY superstore were used in its construction, and staining with tea helped the ageing process.

In 2005, suspicions arose over three Assyrian stone reliefs. The Greenhalghs had tried to use the same provenance as for the Princess – a sales catalogue from an 1892 auction. The reliefs were examined at the British Museum and verified as authentic.

Auction house Bonham's had a look and was not convinced, thinking they were fake. When the British Museum had another look, Irving Finkel, an expert in the early form of

Middle Eastern writing called cuneiform, scrutinized them closely. Finkel noticed a spelling mistake.

The police were called in. After months of investigations, they moved to arrest the family members involved. When they raided the Greenhalgh family home, they found other fakes around the house, including two *Amarna Princesses*.

The police thought Shaun aimed to embarrass the art world in a way similar to that of Tom Keating. He had put in a "tell" – a deliberate fault that should have been spotted straight away, but he was surprised at how often these were consistently missed. The provenance was taken as the primary source for verification.

Shaun and his parents were ordered to pay back the money received from Bolton Museum, and most of it was returned, as Shaun had not spent it. He had not lived a lavish lifestyle on the proceeds of the fakery – reputed to be close to a million pounds. He said he had loved visiting the museum as a youngster and regretted fooling them.

Not all forgeries were recovered, and they remain in circulation. Their current ownership will be added to their provenance, which can only mean they will continue to be sold as authentic. Over time, their real provenance might never be revealed.

ALL AT SEA

Britain has a reputation for being home to famous mariners Francis Drake, Captain Cook, Horatio Nelson and Francis Chichester, who completed a solo round-the-world trip in 1967. One who aimed to emulate them was Donald Crowhurst. When he was presented with the reality that he would come up short, Crowhurst fashioned a scheme that would attempt to deceive.

Crowhurst had had short spells in the Royal Air Force and British Army before starting up his own business, Electron Utilisation, in 1962. He invented an electrical device called the Navicator to assist maritime navigation by detecting beacons. The device worked, but sales were not as high as he'd anticipated.

Thinking of the publicity his business would gain, Crowhurst decided to enter the 1968 *Sunday Times* Golden Globe Race. Entrants sailing yachts would circumnavigate the world single-handedly, non-stop. Chichester's recent achievement had included one stop – this race would go one step further.

Despite only being an amateur sailor, Crowhurst was confident of doing well. Financially, it was a risk, as he'd mortgaged the family home and business to secure funds to acquire a boat and equip it for the race. A local businessman called Stanley Best, who had invested in Crowhurst's business, also put funds into this maritime venture. Of course, there was also a huge physical risk. Crowhurst was married and had four children. He was a weekend sailor. Was this challenge feasible?

The prize on offer was £5,000 for the fastest passage, but Crowhurst was up against accomplished sailors such as Bernard Moitessier and Robin Knox-Johnston. There were no qualifying criteria to enter, so Crowhurst didn't have to prove any sailing prowess beforehand.

Crowhurst wanted to use Francis Chichester's circumnavigating boat *Gipsy Moth IV*, but this was refused. Instead, his boat would be the *Teignmouth Electron*, a trimaran specially built for him and named after the departure port and his own company. This type of boat was fast but difficult to right if capsized. Crowhurst had devised a safety "buoyancy bag" feature on the mast in preparation for such a situation. He hoped that this automatic system, along with others he'd take with him, would become marketable after a successful voyage.

The last chaotic days approaching the race start were filled with Crowhurst equipping his 12-metre-long (40 feet) boat with equipment and provisions, doing publicity and all the other tasks needed. He admitted it wasn't ready, but his sponsors insisted he continue. On the night before departing, Crowhurst tearfully told his wife Clare that the boat wasn't ready. She told him everything would be fine. Preparations ran late, and the *Electron* was the last yacht to sail, right on the last day for the competition entrants to start: 31 October 1968. It sailed without all its safety equipment being 100 per cent ready. Crowhurst said he was going to remedy this when at sea.

FORGERY

As he made his way down the English Channel towards the Atlantic, Crowhurst didn't fall into the water (which he'd done several times when his boat was at Cowes), but he wasn't making very good progress, achieving only half the speed he required.

After only a few weeks into the voyage and off the coast of Portugal, Crowhurst was in trouble. Not only was his boat slow, it was leaking, and the bilge pump wasn't working, so he had to use a bucket to get rid of the water. This boat would not survive the heavy southern seas. Only a few weeks into the voyage, Crowhurst figured he had a 50:50 chance of surviving and thought about abandoning the race, but that way lay financial ruin. Several other competitors had abandoned by this time due to boats being damaged in rough seas.

Just five weeks into the attempt, and with no improvement in sight, he came up with a plan: he would fake it. The *Electron* would not continue round the world but would hold station in the Atlantic then, when the other competitors went past, he would follow on at the end. He would have to falsify his navigational records, but they wouldn't be under much scrutiny compared to the winner's.

As part of his deception, he sent a radio message that he had sailed 243 miles – a record for a solo sailor. He sailed down into the South Atlantic and actually landed in Argentina to buy materials to fix one of his boat's floats. At the same time, the fictional *Electron* was in the Indian Ocean heading east. Crowhurst eventually reached as far south as the Falkland Islands, 8,000 miles from home in March 1969, before turning north.

Crowhurst had spent the past few months in radio silence, as signals would give away his position. He explained it by saying the electrical generator had failed. When he started sending messages again, false positions were sent, which led those following the race to believe he had a chance of winning.

Crowhurst's deceptions had an effect on the other competitors; there were by now only three left. Robin Knox-Johnston had completed the race in April. Nigel Tetley, believing he was up against Crowhurst due to his fictitious position declarations, pushed his boat hard, so much it sunk, and he had to be rescued.

Tetley had actually been in the lead timewise and so threw away his chance of victory needlessly. Crowhurst was now on course to win the fastest journey prize. If he finished first, his logs would be checked over thoroughly by experienced sailors such as Francis Chichester, who had expressed doubt about Crowhurst's progress early in the competition.

As Crowhurst reached the Sargasso Sea, he was confronted with a terrible dilemma: go home and admit his deception or live a lie with all the associated guilt and fear of being uncovered someday in the future. Starting at the end of June, he recorded his thoughts in one of his log books, and they took on a metaphysical nature. He wrote 25,000 words in a week, forming a philosophical view of the world, the cosmos, God's place in them and that of humans.

The last entries were written on 1 July 1969, his two hundred and forty-third day at sea. Among his final words were these: "It is finished – IT IS THE MERCY", which is commonly taken to mean he saw his own end in sight. The *Teignmouth Electron* was found on 10 July, 700 miles west of the Azores. Crowhurst was not on board.

Robin Knox-Johnston, the only finisher of the race, gave his £5,000 prize money to Crowhurst's family. Crowhurst's story has endured as how a person can enter a situation they find impossible to get out of and has been the subject of several documentaries and even a movie starring Colin Firth.

Crowhurst's boat was left to rot on a beach in the Caribbean having, like its owner, never returned to Britain.

TRAVELLERS CHECKS

Born in 1804, Harold Augustus, the Marquis de Bourbel, was charming, polite and skilled with a weapon; he had fatally injured a Greek man in a duel. De Bourbel had been in diplomatic service for France before moving to Florence in Italy in the 1830s. Despite being married with a family, he was no family man – running off with a younger woman when his wife was in her last month of pregnancy. It was said the shock of this betrayal resulted in his wife's death in childbirth.

De Bourbel set up home in Livorno in Tuscany. There, he met up with Scotsman "Wicked" William Cunninghame-Graham, who was not a keen fan of hard work and sobriety; the two got on famously.

They devised a plan to make them a fortune: they would forge letters of credit. These were the nineteenth century equivalent of traveller's cheques. There was one bank, Glyn and Co., that operated differently from others. They did not prewarn banks in Europe when such letters were issued. This allowed the possibility of creating false ones. The continental banks who handed money over would inform Glyn and Co., and the con would fail as there was no money held in the name of the receiver. To succeed, the fraudsters would have to move fast once they had the money.

De Bourbel and Cunninghame-Graham figured that creating many letters for smaller sums wouldn't draw too much attention. They would need multiple agents to present the letters around Europe at the same time.

It was not a simple process to produce the letters. They would need to be printed on special paper and done so without suspicion. They would also have to replicate the banker's signature perfectly. If it worked, the two thought they could bring in £1 million (today's value would be approximately £65 million).

Cunninghame-Graham was technically proficient and had made a tracing machine which was used to copy the signature of one of Glyn and Co.'s partners from a real letter of credit that was being held by a bank where one of Cunninghame-Graham's sons worked.

The enterprise needed more participants. De Bourbel had befriended a man called Frederick Pipe, a surgeon who had married Angelina, a woman once accused of murdering her husband, Thomas Pow, who was a friend of Pipe's. The two were signed up.

Another was Baron Louis D'Arjuzon, a gambling addict who acquired a real letter of credit from Glyn and Co. from which they could make copies. He was accompanied by his mistress, Marie Desjardins.

Others were recruited, including one of Cunninghame-Graham's sons. The wily De Bourbel was not going to be venturing anywhere with a forged document. He had set up an alibi by appearing at the bank where another of Cunninghame-Graham's sons – Allan Bogle – was a partner.

The day of 21 April was when the agents would start visiting banks. Over the next week, they went to Brussels,

Coblenz, Cologne, Florence, Frankfurt, Genoa, Ghent, Liege, Milan, Paris, Parma, Rome, Trieste, Turin and Venice.

It didn't go exactly to plan. One of the gang, Count Charles de Pindray, successfully withdrew several amounts, but after Trieste, he disappeared with the money. Things were going to get worse for the fraudsters.

On 23 April, Thomas Perry, the printer of the 200 letters prepared in advance, was in Antwerp. When he asked for £750 from a banker called Mr Agie, the Belgian was suspicious, as the Englishman had just withdrawn the same amount the previous day and was supposedly heading back to Britain. Why would he need such a sum when he could obtain it more easily back home?

Perry and Angelina Pipe, who was accompanying him, were arrested returning to London. Perry spilled the beans, naming all the other members of the gang.

Realizing things were going south, De Bourbel made his way to Spain. The game was up for all the fraudsters when, on 26 May, *The Times* newspaper published an article with the headline "Extraordinary and Extensive Forgery and Swindling Conspiracy on the Continent". It was not the snappiest headline ever, but it told the story.

Allan Bogle, who had returned to London from Florence, sued the newspaper for libel. The paper's lawyer investigated the events. He found the tracing machine and made a copy of it, which was shown in court. He visited the bankers who had paid out on the letters of credit. The paper's defence was to be that the article was stating the truth. Despite this, Bogle won his case and was awarded damages of one farthing. The jury did not have proof he was one of the conspirators but plainly felt he was not completely innocent.

Perry and Angelina Pipe were found guilty of fraud. They were given hard labour prison sentences and were to be branded. D'Arjuzon and his mistress Marie Desjardins faced trial for forgery in Paris. D'Arjuzon was acquitted, with Desjardins testifying on his behalf, saying he knew nothing of the deception. However, Marie was found guilty and given five years in jail.

It is thought de Bourbel ended up in Texas, and his co-conspirator Cunninghame-Graham stayed in Europe. They escaped any trial.

CORKED

Wine has provided much enjoyment for centuries. A good vintage, with a beautifully prepared meal, is one of life's great pleasures. The choice of wine is almost limitless, with the grape, year of production and the vineyard all playing key parts in what ends up on the table. To make your choices easier, wine experts can advise on what wine matches your taste, your menu choice and – perhaps most importantly – your budget.

However, wine experts are not always right on the money. They can be fooled. As Rudy Kurniawan proved.

Kurniawan claimed it was 2000 when he sipped his first wine in San Francisco. He soon became a fan of Californian-produced wines. He developed his knowledge so much that he was able to mingle with established wine fans in three Los Angeles tasting clubs. It took money to share the company of successful Hollywood figures like Arthur Sarkissian (producer of *Rush Hour* and films starring Samuel L. Jackson and Michael Keaton) and TV director Jef Levy. It also took a high degree of knowledge to perform well at tasting events, something Kurniawan did well.

Kurniawan drove a Ferrari and a Bentley. He wore tailor-made suits. He had money. Lots of it. He wasn't always forthcoming about where the money came from but said he was given a million-dollar allowance per month for buying wine. Or it might have been two million. His family were wealthy from distributing beer (sometimes Heineken, other times it was Guinness) in China. He was brought up in Indonesia; his father had Chinese heritage but had given him an Indonesian surname. Kurniawan explained that this was done to preserve his identity and to give him autonomy.

In October 2004, Kurniawan and some friends embarked on a wine-drinking binge that lasted four days. They drank famous wines such as the 1945 Chateau Mouton Rothschild, 1961 Jaboulet Hermitage La Chapelle and a 1964 Domaine de la Romanée-Conti. Kurniawan was so well-known for his affection for the wines of the latter estate that he was given the nickname "Dr Conti".

These were expensive wines, costing thousands of dollars each. It was claimed by one of those taking part that the cost of the session cost a quarter of a million dollars. Kurniawan asked the staff at the restaurant to keep the empty bottles for him. It wasn't the only time he would request to take bottles home, claiming he was collecting for a wine museum.

Kurniawan was an avid collector of wine and amassed thousands of bottles, especially Burgundies. He would spend millions of dollars at auctions, consistently outbidding others, which helped to push prices up. Once raised to a high level, he then sold off large amounts of his collection, making sizeable profits.

The buying and selling of expensive wines originated in the 1990s with the dot-com boom when fortunes could be made by entrepreneurs starting internet-based companies or by investors who'd seen their projects sold off at a large profit.

In January 2006, the sale of Kurniawan's wines called "the Cellar" brought in $10.6 million. Nine months later, Cellar II took in $24.7 million – a record for an auction sale of a collection owned by one person.

In April 2008 at a wine auction in New York, Kurniawan had put up over 250 bottles of Burgundy for sale. He was selling bottles from three well-regarded Burgundy producers: Domaine Armand Rousseau, Domaine Georges Roumier and Domaine Ponsot.

However, during the auction, Kurniawan's 97 bottles from one winery were removed from sale. Laurent Ponsot, proprietor of Domaine Ponsot, had flown from France to be at the auction. He had suspicions about the veracity of what was being put on sale in his family business's name. For example, there were bottles of Clos Saint-Denis dating from the years 1945 to 1971. The trouble was that the winery had not produced any bottles of this grand cru wine until the 1980s. There were other inconsistencies with other bottles. With counterfeit wines in his domaine's name and the potential damage to its name, Ponsot wanted to find out who was behind this attempted fraud.

Others started to have doubts. One collector, billionaire Arthur Koch, hired a private investigator. He sued Kurniawan in 2009, alleging that he sold him counterfeit wines in 2005 and 2006 via the auction house Acker Merrall & Condit.

In March 2012, Kurniawan was arrested by the FBI. At his Los Angeles suburban home, the agents found what appeared to be a counterfeit wine factory: empty bottles, bottles being soaked in water to allow label removal, old corks, corking tools, rubber stamps with winery names and thousands of labels for Burgundy and Bordeaux wines. Notes were lying around with how to create a blend of wines to imitate the originals. Kurniawan had bought up old wines from a seller in France and had used these to blend with other wines to put in the counterfeit bottles.

During the investigations and the pretrial indictment, it was found that Kurniawan's real name was Zhen Wang Huang. The name "Rudy Kurniawan" was shared with a famous Indonesian badminton player. Kurniawan had been ordered to voluntarily leave the country in 2003 after failing to achieve political asylum after his student visa had expired. He had then remained in the US as an illegal immigrant.

Despite his apparent wealth and wine sales in the tens of millions, it was revealed that he had run out of money and had to borrow over $11 million from Acker Merrall & Condit and a bank in New York. He had defaulted on these loans. He had then borrowed $2 million from fellow wine collectors. In 2007, he sent $17 million back to his brothers in Hong Kong and Indonesia.

With the thousands of bottles of wine having been produced, some of his friends doubted the disorganized Kurniawan was capable of such thorough counterfeiting nor had the time to complete them.

He was charged with wire and mail fraud. As well as the wine offences, he had made a fraudulent claim for a financial loan. As part of this, he claimed artworks from the likes of Andy Warhol and Damien Hirst as collateral for one loan when he had already used them in this way for another.

He was found guilty at trial in New York federal court in December 2013. Kurniawan was given ten years in jail and ordered to forfeit $20 million and pay $28.4 million in restitution. He was deported to Indonesia after his release from prison in 2021. A documentary about Kurniawan called *Sour Grapes* claimed that there were 10,000 fake wines by him still in circulation.

Before sentencing, Kurniawan had apologized and said, "Wine became my life, and I lost myself in it."

DUTCH MASTER

No account of forgers could leave out Han van Meegeren, the Dutch artist who faced trial for collaboration with the Nazis.

Van Meegeren was born in 1889 in Deventer, a small city in the Netherlands. He wanted to be an artist from a young age, but his schoolteacher father thought otherwise, and van Meegeren was to study architecture. He attended college in Delft, which was the hometown of acclaimed seventeenth-century painter Johannes Vermeer. Vermeer was active in the Dutch Golden Age – a span of years from 1588 to 1672 when the Netherlands enjoyed a period of prosperity which saw art and science flourish.

Van Meegeren didn't make it as an architect, dropping out of college in 1913. He moved to The Hague and took art classes, resulting in him working as an assistant to an art professor teaching drawing and art history. Van Meegeren became a full-time artist in 1917. He gained a level of success, rewarded with an exhibition of his work in the city, which was well received.

Five years later, he exhibited again with religious paintings, but this did not garner the same level of praise from the critics. Following a similar pattern to other art forgers, the skilful artist took up arms (and brushes) against the art establishment. He said later, "Driven into a state of anxiety and depression due to the all-too-meagre appreciation of my work, I decided, one fateful day, to revenge myself on the art critics and experts by doing something the likes of which the world had never seen before."

However, it appears that it was not the indifference to his second exhibition that turned him towards forgery – he had been doing it for a while. Van Meegeren is thought to have started creating his own forgeries around 1920. He needed the money to provide for his family.

He was advised and tutored on this line of artwork by a forger and dealer called Theo van Wijngaarden. Van Wijngaarden had learnt from infamous dealer Leonardus Nardus. Nardus had sold recreations and freshly painted old works "by" renowned artists to wealthy Americans in the years around the end of the nineteenth century and the start of the twentieth century.

One of those he'd duped was a millionaire businessman called P. A. B. Widener. When a group of experts looked at Widener's art collection, they thought it worth a twentieth of what he'd paid for it. Nardus was not exposed as it would cause embarrassment to his victim.

Van Meegeren spent years gaining expertise in the right techniques. To create these fakes old paintings were acquired, with authentic period frames and canvas. They were then painted over, using only the pigments that were of the intended period. Ageing techniques to mimic the crackling of the paint were applied, along with yellowed varnish. To achieve the hardening of the paint – something that normally takes half a century – van Meegeren experimented with different techniques. He found that if he mixed the synthetic resin Bakelite with the pigments rather than using oil, this would achieve the desired result after being put in an oven. This limited the size of any work he could produce. He wasn't always careful. For the painting *Christ and the Adulteress,* he used cobalt blue, a pigment that wasn't introduced until the nineteenth century.

His "Vermeers" included works *The Lacemaker* and *The Smiling Girl.* The latter took inspiration from the real Vermeer's *The Girl with a Glass of Wine*, with the amused girl similar to the one imbibing. Both were sold to the American banker Andrew Mellon, who donated them to the National Gallery of Art in Washington, D. C.

In 1937, his painting *The Supper at Emmaus* was accepted as a genuine Vermeer and sold for half a million Dutch guilders – equivalent to around $5 million in today's money. It was exhibited in the Museum Boijmans Van Beuningen. The proceeds were enough to buy van Meegeren a house in the South of France.

Van Meegeren had been married in his early 20s, but not long after arriving in The Hague, he met actor Johanna de Boer. They married in 1928. Van Meegeren enjoyed a hedonistic lifestyle that resulted in his alcohol dependence. It was claimed he kept a house in Amsterdam just for hosting parties.

Van Meegeren was on the right-wing of politics and anti-Semitic. In 1945, after the war had ended, a book of poems by a Dutch Nazi was found in the Reich Chancellery in Berlin. The volume was illustrated by van Meegeren and personally signed and dedicated, "To my beloved Führer in grateful tribute". Van Meegeren accepted the signature was his but claimed the dedication was by a German officer. The handwriting seemed to match both parts.

Soon after the war ended, he faced charges of treason, for selling Dutch national treasures in the form of Vermeer paintings to members of the Nazi hierarchy. One painting, *Christ with the Adulteress* ended up in the hands of *Reichsmarshal* Hermann Göring.

Facing the possibility of the death penalty for collaboration, van Meegeren admitted he had forged the paintings. One expert, who faced losing face and his reputation, refused to accept this and continued to regard the paintings as genuine.

On trial, van Meegeren claimed that he made the forgeries to prove to himself he could do it. When challenged on why he then sold them for high prices, he said he had to, or people would know they were fakes. This brought laughter to the court.

To prove he was behind the paintings, van Meegeren painted a "new" Vermeer under the watchful eye of reporters and witnesses appointed by the court. The work contains an anachronism: Jesus is depicted reading a bible. It was his last Vermeer.

Van Meegeren had claimed that by exchanging his painting for over a hundred genuine Dutch works in Göring's possession, he was doing the country a service. He was seen as a national hero for this and for fooling the Nazis with his fakes. He was given a jail sentence of one year for fraud and had to forfeit the money he'd made.

As a result of the publicity and the trial, van Meegeren's paintings increased in value. Along with others, his son Jacques created fake van Meegerens that fetched higher prices than his own original work.

The master forger died of heart failure in prison a couple of months into his sentence.

A MAN CALLED FLINT JACK

Flint Jack was just one of the names by which a famous nineteenth-century forger was known. Officially, he was Edward Simpson, but he was also Edward Jackson, John Wilson, Jerry Taylor, Bones, Cockney Bill, Fossil Willy, the Old Antiquarian and Shirtless.

He was born in 1815 in the village of Sleights, not far from the English town of Whitby and north Yorkshire's Jurassic coast. He was regarded as a bright child, and when he was 14 years old, he gained a place in service to Dr Young, a local historian and geologist in Whitby. He then worked for a Dr Ripley. From these learned gentlemen Simpson gained a great level of knowledge of archaeology and geology. They also showed him practical skills when they went on field trips to find flints and fossils, which they could then sell. Simpson's keen mind took it all in, and by his mid-20s, he became an expert, earning the nickname "Flint Jack".

When Ripley died in 1840, Simpson was cast loose and began his wanderings. He was able to earn a good living finding and selling fossils to collectors in towns such as Whitby, Scarborough and Filey.

In 1843, he was asked by a Whitby-based dealer if he could copy a barbed arrowhead, the type made by prehistoric peoples for hunting. Simpson converted his knowledge and abilities into crafting one, the raw material flint not being difficult to find in that part of the country. The arrowhead sold. Simpson could make 50 a day.

He also made axe heads and told prospective buyers he'd found them in burial mounds. Simpson also turned his hand to making urns used by the Romans and early Britons. These sold well.

When he had saturated the market in an area, Simpson upped faking tools and moved, pushing his possessions in a wheelbarrow. He applied his metalworking skills to a tin tea tray he found and produced a Roman breastplate. He doubted anyone would fall for it, but one did. As there was lucrative interest in the Roman period, Simpson fashioned a stone milestone that was purchased by a collector in Scarborough. It was said to have eventually entered the British Museum's collection.

In 1846, as well as a taste for forging ancient artefacts, Simpson had found a taste for beer, for which his faking works provided the funds. Speaking in 1866 about this time, Simpson said, "Until then, I was always possessed of five pounds. I have since been in utter poverty and frequently in great misery and want."

When he failed to get authentication for a stone he had found and into which he'd engraved the name of the fourth-century Roman emperor Constantine, along with the Christian ichthys symbol, Simpson was on his way again. He headed south to Peterborough, finding legitimate work with a fossil collector.

The lure was too much, and eventually Simpson created another ancient relic, this time turning a piece of stolen fossilized wood into an abbot's thirteenth-century ring. With its provenance explained as being found by a labourer working at an abbey, the valuable ring was sold to a collector. Simpson did not feel too bad about supplying fake antiquities for collectors as he felt they were still attractive objects in their own right.

Next on Simpson's itinerary was the Essex town of Colchester, where he arrived in 1848. He recruited a salesman who could get his manufactured flints into the hands of London collectors. He didn't dare try anything of a higher value as it would face greater scrutiny. Forging ahead on his own, he moved to London and was able to get many pieces accepted by the curators at the British Museum.

Fearing exposure for the number of flints on the market, he didn't linger in the capital and made his way north to York, where he gained a legitimate position collecting fossils for York Museum, staying there a year.

Next up was the Lake District, where he remained legit, selling amber jewellery and wood carvings, though sometimes a manufactured flint arrowhead would also be sold. Across the Irish Sea, Simpson was able to sell Celtic artefacts like hammers, spears and arrowheads before he made his way back to London in 1852.

Over the next decade, Simpson continued travelling around the country through the Midlands, the West Country and reaching the north country: Scotland. He barely covered his expenses, finding the Scots not easily fooled – they were too "canny".

They were not as careful with their money in Cambridge, where he did a good trade. In Salisbury, he attempted to sell fake flints, but they were spotted immediately by the curator of the local museum. The curator asked Simpson to make a set of flints, displayed under a label warning "to the unwary" to avoid being duped.

In 1861, Simpson was back in London with Professor Tennant, a geology expert. When enquiries were made by Tennant as to his activities, Simpson admitted he had been making and selling fake items. Tennant didn't turn him in to the authorities but said he would introduce Simpson to several archaeological and geologists' clubs if he displayed his skills, showing how he created his forgeries. This exposure meant the end of Simpson's fakery career.

With his drinking requiring more and more money, Simpson made some bad decisions. In January 1867, he stayed in Bedford with his friend James Wyatt, the respected archaeologist and editor of a local newspaper he had known for several years. Simpson knew Wyatt's knowledge and experience made him a difficult person to pass off any of his forgeries and so didn't attempt to.

Simpson was given money and clothes by Wyatt to help him make his way to London. Simpson's fondness for imbibing meant he spent all his money in a pub and, when that was gone, sold the clothes he'd been given. He then tried to gain more money by stealing a barometer from a house and a clock from a chapel.

When caught and found guilty, he was lucky to avoid transportation to the British colonies and instead was given a year in jail. Another spell in jail resulted in 1869 from what a local newspaper described as a "fossil felony" in Whitby and saw him given six weeks hard labour. A few years later, he spent more time in jail after stealing a topcoat from a geologist in North Yorkshire. Simpson took the coat despite being given money by the man.

FORGERY

Simpson is last recorded as having been seen in 1874, at another appearance in the dock in front of the magistrates, this time at Malton in North Yorkshire. It is thought he may have ended his days penniless in a Victorian workhouse a few years after. As happens often with a master forger, Simpson's works are nowadays sought after as collectable pieces. A newspaper in 1871 described Simpson as "a notorious vendor of spurious antiquities", which described succinctly his forging career but failed to mention his skills and talent as a craftsman.

INVESTMENT FRAUD

To "get rich quick" appeals to many. Schemes that, to a calm, rational mind, appear unrealistic can be attractive to those caught up in the fear of missing out.

The "Ponzi scheme" (where the first investors get paid from the money invested by later investors) promised huge profits to the citizens of Boston who raced to give the originator, Charles Ponzi, their money. There were 40,000 of them: businessmen, politicians, clergymen and police officers, all alongside ordinary members of the public.

When the scheme collapsed, it sent a message to others to be careful where they put their own money – or did it? In the US in 2019, authorities found 60 large-scale Ponzi schemes, with over $3 billion being invested in this type of scam. It seems that the appetite for losing your money is as strong as ever.

Another type of investment fraud is insider trading. Using "non-public" information to gain a trading advantage in selling or buying stocks and shares is illegal. There are many cases of insider trading, and even the famous can fall foul of the law. American TV personality Martha Stewart was jailed in 2004 for actioning information that saw her sell $230,000 of shares in a biopharmaceutical company before their value dropped.

There are some other high-profile cases of investment fraud that you'll read about in the following pages.

STOCK IN TRADE

London's Stock Exchange dates back to the sixteenth century, when its predecessor, the Royal Exchange, was opened, appropriately, by Queen Elizabeth I. Initially, stockbrokers were banned from entering due to their rude behaviour and lack of manners.

By the start of the nineteenth century, the Stock Exchange had a new building, which, in 1814, was to be the scene of memorable events.

Not long after midnight on the morning of 21 February, a man dressed in military uniform entered an inn in Dover on England's south-east coast. He said he had just arrived from France and had news of great national importance. The man asked for a pen and paper in order to write a message bearing this news. The dispatch was to go to Admiral Foley, who was a short distance along the coast at Deal.

The officer also asked for a carriage and horses to take him to London. These were provided. The officer had offered to pay in "Napoleons" – gold coins named after France's ruler and chief enemy of Britain. When these were refused, he paid with pound notes (which he said he'd had for a while). Despite having suffered a defeat in Russia in 1812, Napoleon was still a much-feared commander.

The officer wrote that Napoleon was dead, killed by Russian Cossacks, who had cut up his corpse. Cossacks were highly effective cavalrymen who had fought well against Napoleon's forces in their attack on Russia. They had almost caught Napoleon in the French retreat, but now it seemed they had succeeded. The Allies were in Paris. Peace was assured.

This was monumental news. The officer, who gave his rank and name as Lieutenant Colonel du Bourg, got into the carriage and headed to the capital. His message was delivered to Admiral Foley at three in the morning.

The news spread quickly, and by the time the Stock Exchange opened for business at 10 a.m., there was great excitement. When trading started, government stocks (what we would know as interest-paying bonds) rose in value. However, official confirmation had not been issued. The price then started to fall.

It was to rally after an intervention by other officers. Three men wearing blue overcoats and white cockades – the symbol of the deposed French royal house of Bourbon – were seen in a carriage riding into London, shouting "*Vive le roi!*" (Long live the king!) With this further spreading of the news of Bonaparte's passing, the stock price rose again.

Later that afternoon, news came that the French emperor was not dead. Lieutenant Colonel du Bourg's pound notes were found to have been issued in London less than a week before. He was an imposter. As were the French royal supporters in the London carriage.

Du Bourg's movements were traced, and it turned out that once in London, he'd gone to an address in Grosvenor Square – the residence of Lord Thomas Cochrane. Cochrane was a famed naval commander in the Napoleonic wars.

(He later inspired the fictional characters of maritime adventure novels, Horatio Hornblower and Jack Aubrey.) Cochrane was popular with the public but had made enemies in his attempts to reform Parliament and the Admiralty, which he accused of corruption.

Cochrane's uncle was Andrew Cochrane Johnstone, and on the morning of 21 February, Cochrane had breakfasted with his uncle at his uncle's home in Cumberland Street, along with Richard Butt – their stockbroker. Later that morning, Cochrane returned to his house where he met with du Bourg – who was actually Charles Random de Berenger, a man he already knew through making architectural drawings for his uncle. De Berenger was from Prussia and had served in the British Army. He was £350 in debt and asked Cochrane to give him a position as a sharpshooter on his naval warship, the *Tonnant*. This was not easy to secure because he was a foreign national. Although he was upset, de Berenger would have to wait.

The Stock Exchange Committee quickly worked out that there had been a deliberate attempt to defraud. They found that three people had sold their stock on the tumultuous day: Thomas Cochrane, his uncle Andrew Cochrane Johnstone and Richard Butt. They had made a profit of over ten thousand pounds – equivalent in today's money to around half a million pounds.

While Cochrane was not that interested in the machinations of stocks, his uncle Cochrane Johnstone (who had a shady past, which included swindling Spain out of paying money for rifles it never received) very much was and, when Cochrane Johnstone had seen an opportunity to manipulate the price through fake news of Napoleon's death, he took it, encouraging de Berenger to buy the uniform and go to Dover to start the ruse.

Cochrane Johnstone had told de Berenger he faced financial ruin, having bought much government stock. He needed the stock's price to go up.

When it was over, Cochrane Johnstone told him he was sure to be a scapegoat and urged him to flee. De Berenger tried to get to Europe but was arrested in Leith in Scotland and brought back to the capital.

On 8 June, Cochrane, Cochrane Johnstone and Butt were put on trial for conspiracy alongside those accused of pretending to be officers proclaiming the news on the morning of 21 June. They were all found guilty. Before any sentence could be carried out, Cochrane Johnstone fled Britain, never to return.

Cochrane and Butt were fined £1,000 each and sent to prison for a year. They were also sentenced to stand in the pillory – a wooden structure with holes for the head and hands – for an hour each day, but this humiliation was later removed from their punishment. Cochrane was thrown out of the navy and lost his seat in Parliament, although he was soon re-elected. He proclaimed his innocence until his death in 1860.

De Berenger, who wrote often to Cochrane looking for assistance, was given a year in prison. He died in 1845, in debt.

THE GREAT PONZI

Some attain long-lasting fame by having a great achievement named after them. You only have to think of the Fosbury Flop or the Panenka penalty to be reminded of how Dick Fosbury created a new way of clearing the high jump bar or how Czech footballer Antonín Panenka lofted his penalty kick over a despairing goalkeeper with the deftest of touches.

A "Ponzi scheme" refers to a fraud whereby payments from current investors fund the financial returns of previous investors. Of course, investors don't know it is a Ponzi scheme – all they see are promised high rates of return.

The fraudster makes their money by charging high fees from the investors or just takes the money and disappears. The scheme always runs the risk of the fraudster not being able to service the initial investments by not securing enough new deposits.

The concept of "robbing Peter to pay Paul" goes back centuries, but the name of this scam stems from a man called Charles Ponzi, an Italian who plied his trade in the US. Born in 1882, he came from a family that had once been part of the aristocracy, and he promised his mother he'd restore their wealth and status.

Ponzi went to university in Rome but spent his money enjoying student life and didn't trouble the library too much.

He worked for a while as a postal worker in Italy before emigrating to the US in 1903 to make his fortune. The ambitious Ponzi arrived with only $2.50 to his name. He'd gambled away the rest of his money on the voyage: $200 his family had scraped together to get him off to a good start.

After several years, Ponzi hadn't made his fortune. After trying a few jobs here and there, Ponzi made it to Montreal, Canada, where he started working in a bank used by Italian immigrants. The owner had promised his customers a higher rate of interest than the other banks. To pay them, he used new deposits to pay the interest due earlier investors. When the bank eventually failed, the owner absconded to Mexico with a large amount of his company's money. The idea of using fresh money to pay existing commitments was not to be forgotten by Ponzi.

Without a job, Ponzi was short of money. He tried forging cheques from former clients of the bank, but he was caught and sent to Canadian prison for three years. Another spell in prison in the US for smuggling illegal Italian immigrants into the country quickly followed in 1911.

After a couple of failed businesses, Ponzi tried another tack. In January 1920, he formed the Securities Exchange Company in Boston, whose basis would be buying international reply coupons. These coupons were created by the United States Postal Service. A sender could prepurchase postage and send the coupon in their letter. When the recipient received it, they then took it to their post office to exchange for stamps.

Ponzi noticed there could be a price difference. He devised a scheme to buy coupons from countries where they were cheap and then sell them where they had a higher value, thus making a profit on each one. He promised investors they'd receive a 50 per cent return on their investment in just 45 days or double it in 90 days.

It was a popular idea, and investors flocked to get involved and buy their own "Ponzi notes". Ponzi's business grew quickly, with offices being set up in nearby states. Early investors reinvested their money when they'd received their first returns on investment.

The money kept on coming in. Ponzi was making a fortune – $2.5 million was invested in June – allowing him to live in luxury, wearing a diamond tiepin and having a chauffeur-driven limousine. It also allowed him to invest in local banks. One was the Hanover Trust bank (which had refused him money to start his business). He wanted to take it over and bought enough shares to do so.

Could it last?

The issue was simple: there was no trade in coupons. To generate a profit through the reply coupons would require huge amounts of them, something not logistically possible. There were not nearly enough coupons in circulation to generate the profits required. It would need 160 million coupons to produce the required returns; there were only 27,000 in existence. These first investors were being paid from the money received from the next set of those looking for an easy and quick buck.

Ponzi faced a few challenges. Rival schemers set up offices next door, hoping to take business away from those queuing up to invest their money. Plus, a furniture salesman who had sold him office furniture took legal action. He claimed he was a partner in Ponzi's scheme and wanted a million dollars. This legal action froze Ponzi's bank accounts and caused a run on the Securities Exchange Company.

In July, *The Boston Post* newspaper published a series of stories on Ponzi. The Massachusetts banking commissioner wanted to know more. The stakes were then upped when Clarence Barron, the owner of *The New York Times*, questioned just how Ponzi was able to sell so many coupons. He also asked why Ponzi kept his own money in regional banks when there was so much more money to be had in the coupon industry. The district attorney investigated.

Ponzi's scheme was soon to be over. The negative press resulted in a run on the company, which was found to be millions in debt and was declared insolvent.

Ponzi was charged with mail fraud and, in November 1920, was sentenced to five years in prison. Investors lost $20 million in what was described at the time as "the fraud of the century". It was all over in less than a year.

Ponzi served three and a half years behind bars. He was then tried on state charges of larceny three times and was finally found guilty at the third trial. He was given 7–9 years and described as a "common and notorious thief". When released from prison on bail while appealing larceny offences, Ponzi set up a business venture in Florida selling swampland. He tried to flee to Italy but was caught and returned to prison.

Despite earning millions, he eventually died penniless in Brazil in 1948. What was long-lasting was the infamy earned by a man who said, "I had given them the best show."

HOWE IN THE WORLD

Before Charles Ponzi earned his place in the hall of financial infamy, there was another who could have had the scam named in their dishonour: Sarah Howe. Not a lot is known about the background and early life of Howe, but it is known that by 1877, she was in Boston (half a century before Ponzi started his schemes there) and working as a fortune teller, reading cards and selling horoscopes for 25 cents a time.

In 1875, Howe had been arrested for applying for several loans with the same property as collateral. She was sent to jail for a year, but on appeal, her conviction was found to be faulty.

In 1879, Howe formed the Ladies' Deposit Company, where women could have their money deposited and looked after by other women. The women were to be unmarried, not homeowners, and not have anyone else looking after their money; they were to be "unprotected females".

They were certainly unprotected – from being swindled.

Investors were promised great returns: 8 per cent interest per month, with interest paid in advance every three months. Deposits had to be more than $200 but less than $1,000. Word soon spread without any advertising, and the money rolled in from Massachusetts and New England.

Deposits in 1880 were five times those of the previous year. Enough money to cover payments for the interest due to be paid out was acquired in the first quarter of 1880. From the start, Howe told depositors that the company was a charity to help women of modest means, funded by the Quakers, to the tune of a million and a half dollars.

As would happen with Ponzi, some depositors paid back in their profits, thus leaving themselves with all their financial eggs in that one basket. It is thought that around half a million dollars was paid in from over 1,200 women. The scheme grew on the basis of personal referrals, and it was described at one point as a craze where women – many of good status in the community – were desperate to gain entry to the scheme. Larger premises were needed in Boston to house the staff needed to process all the paperwork, and a branch office was opened in the city of New Bedford.

Men were piqued at not being able to find out anything about the company. They were barred from investing or even gaining entry to the bank's premises. In September 1880, men and women found out everything when newspaper stories in the *Boston Advertiser* exposing the scheme led to a run on Howe's bank. New investors thought better of it, and those with money already in, wanted their cash out.

An earlier report in the *Boston Herald* in January that year had seen some withdraw their capital. But others were put off doing this, aware of the condition that if they took out all their money, they wouldn't be allowed to re-enter later.

The scheme was on the same basis as that later carried out by Ponzi: everything runs okay as long as investors keep putting their money in, which pays the returns of the early investors. However, when the new well of money dries up, the foundations crack, and the whole thing collapses. Howe paid out $240,000 in interest and capital in an effort to halt the panic, but it was in vain.

In 1881, Howe, along with her accomplice Julia Gould, was arrested, found guilty and given three years in prison for taking money under false pretences. At the collapse of the company, over 800 depositors were still looking for their money, totalling $290,000. Despite this, when Howe was put on trial, several women backed her up, saying she was the victim of men who were unhappy at seeing a woman becoming successful in business.

Howe had not shown any great signs of achieving such a successful criminal career previous to her time in charge of the "Women's Bank". She was illiterate and, at one time in her life, had been incarcerated in a mental institution for being "insane". But she was clearly clever enough to convince hundreds that their money belonged in her company.

In an American magazine report of 1881, Howe was described as "one of the most exuberant, spontaneous, imaginative, and unnecessary liars that ever breathed".

On her release in 1884, she repeated her strategy and opened a Woman's Bank in Boston, this time offering 7 per cent. She was found out again and took off with $50,000. When apprehended, Howe was not prosecuted as those scammed were too embarrassed to face public exposure in a trial.

Howe returned to fortune telling before dying in 1892. When she died, there was not enough money to pay for a clergyman to perform a funeral service. If only she had seen it coming.

MONTE CARLO AND BUST

While one conman had an illegal scheme named after them, few have had songs composed in their honour. One was Charles Wells, who had a song written after his most famous success, but there was more to Wells's career than what happened in the south of France.

Charles De Ville Wells hailed from England, being born in Hertfordshire in 1841. His family were well-off: his father combined legal work as a lawyer with writing poetry (he had gone to school with John Keats); his mother was the daughter of a schoolteacher.

Not long after he was born, the family moved to France, where his father taught English. When he reached adulthood, Wells worked as an engineer in Marseille's dockyards. Showing an innovative bent, he invented a mechanism that regulated a ship propeller's speed and sold the patent for 5,000 francs. He came up with other ideas, such as a way of making luminous signs, but none delivered a decent financial income.

By 1882, Wells and his wife and child had moved to Paris. That year, Wells ran his first fraudulent scheme, getting Parisians to invest in the Banque Industrielle de France, which would invest in the raw material mining industry. It was commonplace for banks to open up and then close down shortly afterwards. Banks then were not highly regulated, and investors faced losing their money without any chance of recompense. Despite negative press reports, enough money was invested in his new enterprise to allow Wells and his family a move to a grander apartment in the French capital.

Wells then came up with a new scheme to build a railway line in the Pas-de-Calais. It offered returns of over 50 per cent. Investors bought shares in the venture, but not a millimetre of track was ever laid. When the authorities investigated, Wells ran off with the invested money (around a million pounds in today's value) and returned to Britain. In his absence, he was found guilty of fraud.

In Britain, Wells continued to come up with inventions involving mustard preservation, torpedoes, umbrellas, rockets and a method of cleaning ships' hulls. He submitted almost a hundred patents, none of which made him any money. He had spent his gains from the Parisian schemes on these and a collection of boats.

Wells's wife, Marie Thérèse, became disenchanted with her husband through his fraudulent behaviour in France and his lack of income in Britain. She left him and returned to France with their daughter, the unfortunately named Marie Antoinette.

In 1887, Wells moved to London and changed tack: he asked investors to help fund the inventions, from which they would then receive a share of the profits. One proved to be successful – a musical skipping rope – and he sold the patent for £50. Others, not so much.

He spent money on advertisements to encourage investors, placing them in the numerous publications of the day. One of his adverts in the press promised the investment to be better than "a gold mine".

Wells promised large profits to any willing investor. He took money from the offspring of British Army officers, retired doctors and spinsters. He would tailor his pitch depending on their circumstances.

At this point, whether Wells still believed in his ability to make a fortune from his ideas or was scamming from the start remains unknown. As the months went by with nothing of their promised returns arriving, investors began to have suspicions.

In 1890, Wells met a woman who was to have a major impact on his life. Jeannette Pairis was beautiful – an artists' model – and almost 30 years younger than him. Pairis had expensive tastes in clothes, jewellery, food and drink.

To impress his new lover, Wells acquired a cargo ship, the *Tycho Brahe*, which he renamed *Palais Royal*. He needed money to fit it out as a luxury vessel, able to accommodate 50 people in the ballroom.

In the summer of 1891, he visited the casino in Monte Carlo. It was the events that took place here that were to inspire the song "The Man Who Broke the Bank at Monte Carlo". Wells had arrived with £400 (around £40,000 in today's money). On 28 July, at noon, he started playing roulette and card games. He started winning. And didn't stop.

This continued for five days, with Wells sleeping with the money under his pillow. At the end, he had amassed £40,000 (£4 million). He had indeed "broken the bank", as this described a situation where there physically wasn't enough money on the casino floor to pay out the winnings. Play was suspended until more cash was brought from the safe. Wells claimed he did this ten times. It was a remarkable run of good luck. At one point, he defeated the odds and won 23 spins out of 30 on the roulette table.

Was it luck? It could have been. Was it cheating? As an inventor, he could have possibly come up with some device to predict any probability flaws in the roulette wheels. Was it set up to engender publicity for the casino in collusion with the man in charge, Camille Blanc? Possibly. Wells himself claimed he had a system that never failed him.

The following year, after an unsuccessful trip to the same casino, Wells was arrested at Le Havre and extradited to Britain. At the Old Bailey court in London, he was given an eight-year sentence for 23 fraud offences. When in prison, he was serenaded by the public who'd gathered outside, singing "The Man Who Broke the Bank at Monte Carlo" to him. The song had become a popular music hall tune. "Monte Carlo Wells" was released after six years. As a parting gift, he played the song he'd inspired on the prison chapel organ.

Despite time in prison, Wells was not finished with illegal activity. In 1910, as "Lucien Rivier", he established a private Parisian bank. Depositors were promised an interest rate of 365 per cent per year. Six thousand investors deposited two million francs. Those who had paid in at the start received their interest from the funds being paid in by more recent investors.

Wells's venture didn't escape attention, and when the authorities started investigating, "Rivier" took the money and ran back to Britain. His escape was temporary, and in 1912, he was brought back to the French capital and given five years in jail.

Wells died in 1922, owing two weeks' rent.

MADOFF WITH ALL THE MONEY

Of all the names who swindled money in the financial sector, few come more well-known than Bernie Madoff's. He ran the world's biggest-ever Ponzi scheme, estimated at being worth $65 billion, run over many years.

Madoff grew up in the middle-class suburban area of Queens in New York. His father had experienced several business failures, and the young Madoff resolved to make a big success of himself in the centre of the US financial world, Wall Street.

In 1960, after accumulating money through work installing lawn sprinklers and as a lifeguard, Madoff started trading outside of the New York Stock Exchange on "over-the-counter" stocks. This proved to be successful; he then started advising clients on their investments. These clients were referred to him by his father-in-law, who co-owned a successful New York accountancy firm. This side of the business was not made public.

Madoff earned fees from this new line of wealth management business, but in the 1962 crash all his stocks were wiped out. He borrowed $30,000 from his father-in-law to pay back the investors. This made him look like a financial genius, as everyone else had lost money.

In the 1970s, he adapted quickly to using computers in his legitimate stock trading business. This helped start the NASDAQ, the first electronic stock exchange. The more secretive and unregistered wealth management business was still in operation.

The 1980s were boom times for the financial world, with deregulation the mantra. Madoff was seen as a major player – a "master of the universe", as writer Tom Wolfe would describe those titans of Wall Street.

Times were good; Madoff bought a penthouse apartment in Manhattan; he commuted by seaplane from a $4 million home in Long Island. He could also stay on his estate in Palm Beach or, if he wanted a vacation further away, there was the home in the south of France, getting there by private jet.

On Monday, 19 October 1987, bedlam and panic ensued as the markets crashed. Black Monday saw mass selling of stocks. As a "market-maker", Madoff was buying up stocks where he could. This helped earn him a reputation for being trustworthy. He was seen as a reliable figure, described by *The New York Times* as the "senior statesman of Wall Street". He was appointed chairman of NASDAQ and brought in as an expert on committees.

His secretive wealth management operation was, in the 1990s, giving investors up to 19 per cent returns. By this time, the investors were being provided to Madoff via two accountants who had taken over from Madoff's father-in-law: Frank Avellino and Michael Bienes.

In 1992, when the financial authorities became aware of a sales brochure offering "riskless trading", they investigated.

Riskless trading was not something easily achieved on Wall Street or any other financial centre.

The two accountants, Avellino and Bienes, were issued with a small fine and made to pay back the money they'd received from investors. Madoff's staff created a false paper trail, which satisfied the investigating Securities and Exchange Commission (SEC), and no action was taken against him. The SEC investigated Madoff eight times between 1992 and 2008.

Madoff's business grew and grew after he was cleared. People with money or who looked after other's money heard that he was providing steady returns. Madoff's company had initially received investments from friends and family members and those he met through his country club before expanding to see charities and large institutional investors invest large amounts of money.

Needing more space to service its five thousand investors, the secretive and unregistered wealth management operation was moved to the 17th floor of the Lipstick Building, where Madoff's company was based. The activities of this floor were kept separate from the stock-trading business, up on the 19th floor. Staff from the different areas were not encouraged to visit each other or to discuss what they were working on.

When Madoff took on his first hedge fund client, Fairfield Greenwich, he didn't charge fees, which was unusual for these types of funds. He only took a commission. Fairfield invested 95 per cent of a $7.2 billion fund with Madoff. This amounted to half its total capital.

Some pondered why, despite any market fluctuations, Madoff's returns were always consistently higher. One financial expert, Harry Markopolos, submitted to the SEC that there was a possibility Madoff was running a Ponzi scheme. Nothing came of it. After all, Madoff had been investigated several times, and yes, there were press articles questioning his success, but he was this great, successful figure, his reputation built up over years.

In 2008, things changed. With the global financial crisis and resultant widespread anxiety, investors wanted their money out. This was difficult for Madoff as there was a $1.2 billion deficit between what money he had and the clients' withdrawal requests. The game was up. Madoff's two sons, who had run the legitimate part of the business and had only just found out the true nature of the fraud that had been running for years, turned him in to the authorities. Madoff had told his sons it was all "one big lie". This was true: no securities had ever been traded on the 17th floor.

On 11 December 2008, the 70-year-old was arrested. The following year, he pleaded guilty to 11 federal charges, including securities, mail and wire fraud and money laundering. He was sentenced to 150 years in jail and ordered to forfeit $170 billion as restitution.

Madoff's brother Peter, who was chief compliance officer at the trading side of the business, pleaded guilty to tax and securities fraud charges and received a ten-year prison sentence.

While Madoff lost money and his freedom, others suffered worse. A French investment fund manager called René-Thierry Magon de la Villehuchet killed himself days after Madoff was arrested. De la Villehuchet had lost $1.5 billion of his clients' money. Madoff's son Mark died by his own hand two years after his father was arrested. His brother Andrew died of cancer aged 48 in 2014. He had blamed the stresses brought on by the events around his father's business behind the return of the cancer he had successfully battled in 2003.

Madoff died in prison in 2021. After his arrest he had said, "I'm not proud that I did what I did."

INSIDE JOB

Insider trading describes when someone is able to profit from the sale or purchase of company shares with knowledge that is not publicly available. They gain an advantage in knowing if the share value is going to increase or decrease and make their trades accordingly. It is illegal, but it wasn't always.

Albert H. Wiggin became president of the Chase National Bank in 1911. In 1917, he became chief executive officer and chairman of the board of directors. Under his competent leadership, the bank grew by increasing its deposits and number of shareholders and acquiring other banks. By 1931, the bank's assets amounted to $2.7 billion, up from a hundred million just 20 years before. It was the largest bank in the world. Wiggin was so well-regarded he appeared on the cover of *Time* magazine.

Wiggin was an influential and respected figure through the 1920s and further enhanced his reputation during Black Thursday (24 October) of the Wall Street Crash of 1929. As the stock market collapsed, Wiggin and other bank senior officials committed $130 million to buy shares above the market price in US companies, thus steadying the ship, at least for a while.

The man who walked onto the floor of the New York Stock Exchange to buy these shares (starting with US Steel) was Richard Whitney, the acting president of the exchange. Despite these efforts, the downward trend continued. In 1932, stocks were worth 89 per cent less than in 1929. The Great Depression followed, resulting in high unemployment and economic hardship for millions around the world.

Wiggin was praised for his actions.

A US Senate inquiry investigated the Wall Street Crash, with Ferdinand Pecora, a former New York district attorney, as chief counsel. Under his probing questioning, they uncovered the fact that Wiggin – along with other banking officials – was able to short sell bank shares in the weeks leading up to the Crash. Short selling is when shares are borrowed, sold at a high price, then when the price drops, shares are bought back and returned to the lender. The seller pockets the profit. Wiggin sold over 40,000 shares. He was able to do this using shell companies based in Canada, owned by him and his family members, to do the buying and selling and, by doing so, avoiding paying tax on the income. He made a $4 million profit when others were losing everything.

Exploiting this conflict of interest, in wishing to see a drop in the value of his own bank's shares, made him unpopular, but he had done nothing illegal. Financial regulations were brought in to prevent it from happening again.

In an unwelcome legacy, the 1934 Securities Exchange Act contained the "Wiggin Provision", making sure that company directors were unable to short sell their own company's stock and thus profit when it was on the slide.

Pecora said, "In the entire investigation, it is doubtful if there was another instance of a corporate executive who so thoroughly and successfully used his official and fiduciary position for private profit." As the regulations couldn't be applied retrospectively, there were no criminal charges that could be applied. But Wiggin did not get off scot-free. In 1933, he was forced out, standing down from his position as chairman of the bank's board. He had to forego his company pension of $100,000 a year.

Wiggin wasn't the only major figure in the attempt to prevent the Crash of 1929 who lost out. Richard Whitney, who had fronted the attempt to shore up the market and earned the nickname the "White Knight of Wall Street", wasn't to remain a respected figure. After losing money investing in an alcoholic beverage company, he took money from pension funds. He faced charges of embezzlement and was jailed in 1938.

Wiggin had acquired a large collection of books and fine art and donated these to public institutions. One gift of five thousand items to the Boston Public Library included works by Rembrandt, Albrecht Dürer and Whistler. He died in 1951.

NADEL AND THE DAMAGE DONE

Arthur Nadel died in prison in 2012, aged 79. He was incarcerated in the Federal Correctional Complex in Butner, North Carolina. A fellow inmate of that jail was a certain Bernie Madoff. The two shared a criminal approach to funding their lifestyles. Both ran Ponzi schemes that defrauded hundreds of investors of millions of dollars: $168 million in Nadel's case.

The "Mini-Madoff", as he nicknamed himself, graduated with a law degree from New York University but was disbarred in 1982 for misappropriating money held in an escrow account – even though he paid back the money plus interest.

He moved to Florida in the mid-1980s and worked in several sectors, including retail, real estate and finance. At one point in the 1990s, he earned an income from playing the piano in a family restaurant. In that decade, Nadel and his future wife Peg set up a day-trading investment club called Inside Scoop. Using computer programming to spot trends on the NASDAQ stock exchange, the venture was a success. Other clubs were established, but this would not end his ambitions – Nadel moved on to bigger and better things.

This came after Nadel met with Neil Moody, a vice president at Wall Street finance company Paine Webber, in 1998. Moody was keen to tap into the success of Nadel's trading acumen. The two set up a fund called Valhalla Investment Partners. There would be five others: Scoop Real Estate, Victory IRA Fund, Victory Fund, Viking IRA Fund and Viking Fund, managed by a new company called Scoop Management. Neil's son Chris also joined the enterprise.

In classic Ponzi style, Nadel would tell investors that he was successful in trading and the resultant funds were higher in value than they were in reality. He told them his yearly returns were in double-digits – up to 55 per cent at one point. He was not telling the truth. He consistently lost money and needed to gain new investors, attracted by these high rates of return so that he could pay the early inventors.

Nadel took large fees based on these inflated figures. He invested in a range of legitimate businesses and real estate properties (including two airfields). He bought five aircraft. The Nadels were also generous supporters of multiple charities in the Sarasota area and were given awards for their generosity.

Nadel claimed the funds he controlled had assets of $300 million, but in reality, they were worth just a bit less: less than $1 million. In total, Nadel's Ponzi schemes raised more than $330 million from almost 400 investors. They ran for ten years until 2009.

The crash of 2008 made investors nervous, and the supply of new investment money dried up. In January 2009, when clients wanted to see financial statements, Nadel disappeared, leaving his wife what appeared to be a suicide note. The 76-year-old went on a 13-day vacation, living it up in New

Orleans and San Francisco. Before disappearing, he had transferred $1.25 million into a secret bank account. On his return to Florida, he gave himself up to the FBI.

In February 2010, Nadel pleaded guilty to 15 counts of securities, mail and wire fraud. He was given a 14-year prison sentence and ordered to forfeit $162 million, his real estate properties and six aircraft for what was described as "the largest Ponzi scheme in Southwest Florida history". The Moodys faced civil securities fraud charges, which they settled, and were barred from working with securities for five years.

The US Attorney who prosecuted the case against him, Preet Bharara from the Southern District of New York, said after the sentencing, "He cheated his elderly and unwitting victims out of their retirement savings and consigned others to poverty."

Before his sentencing, 96 of those he defrauded, most of them retirees, made victim statements. Some were financially wiped out. One, who had lost all his savings of $250,000, said, "I am broke. I need every penny I have just to exist until I die."

After Nadel's death in 2012, one retired man who'd lost $800,000 said, "I can't say I grieve for him. I do wish that he would have had more time to contemplate his crimes."

MAVRODI TO RUIN

Sergei Mavrodi was born in Moscow in the middle of the Cold War, in 1955. He attended the Moscow Institute of Electronics and Mathematics and emerged as a software engineer.

The decline and fall of the communist Soviet Union at the end of the 1980s gave more freedom to entrepreneurs and in 1989, Mavrodi started a company called MMM – the name from the founders' surnames: Mavrodi, his brother and his brother's wife Olga Melnikova. It was a cooperative that imported personal computers to Russia. He also sold pirated audio and video cassettes. Mavrodi did so well that he gave a television address on New Year's Eve and paid for residents of Moscow to have free travel on the city's Metro.

In the early 1990s, he changed tack and started a financial investment operation. On 1 February 1994, shares were issued costing 1,000 rubles each. By July, they were at 125,000 rubles. Investors were promised enticing, if somewhat unbelievable, returns: 3,000 per cent a year.

Their investment would go into companies that had been privatized following the abandonment of the socialist system. As seen in other get-very-rich-quick schemes, the returns came from the Ponzi format – paying off earlier investors with money received from newer ones. No proper investments were made in the former state-owned enterprises.

It is estimated that up to 15 million Russians invested in MMM. Even when it became known that it was a Ponzi scheme, they kept putting their money in, as some investors were making large profits, and others hoped to join them. A series of popular TV adverts showing a normal Russian man who becomes rich as a result of investing with MMM helped attract more investors.

Mavrodi said in 1994, "It was impossible to count the money, we estimated it by eye, by the roomful." The power suits of American financial figures were in contrast to what Mavrodi wore: tracksuits and polo shirts. He was also different in his stated aims. He said he wanted to help the people by buying up these privatized state properties that could have fallen into the hands of the oligarchs.

When he was denied being able to issue new shares, he printed "Mavros", MMM coupons which resembled ruble banknotes, but instead of Lenin's face, Mavrodi had his own face appearing on the paper. Purchasers could sell them back – hopefully for a profit – but there were fewer offices buying them than selling them.

Unhappy with his activities, in 1994, the Russian authorities accused him of tax evasion. Unlike in the US, Ponzi schemes were not illegal in Russia as financial regulation had not been developed as it emerged from a socialist economy. Mavrodi was arrested. Aware of the immunity from prosecution if elected, he stood as a deputy to the State Duma, the lower house of Russia's parliament. Investors thought Mavrodi would have a better chance of paying back their investments if he wasn't in jail, so they voted him in. Mavrodi never attended any parliamentary sittings and so lost this immunity in 1996.

MMM had been unable to keep paying out its high interest rates, and it crashed, being declared bankrupt in 1997. Millions of Russians lost everything. It has been estimated that investors in Mavrodi's schemes lost as much as $1.5 billion, although some who withdrew their money early enough did make a profit. It was also thought that around 50 people died through illness or suicide as a result of losing all their money. Mavrodi was not too concerned, stating that they were adults who knew what they were getting into.

He went into hiding but, after seven years, was tracked down to a rented Moscow apartment. In 2003, he was arrested and put on trial for financial fraud. In April 2007, he was sentenced to four and a half years in a penal colony but had time served in custody before his trial and so was released the following month.

On his release from federal jail, Mavrodi was met with flowers from supporters and sour cream being thrown by his detractors. One woman there said, "I lost a lot, I'm still paying my debts, I almost lost my apartment, but I have no grudge against him. I had a big tragedy in the family, but I don't blame him."

While hiding, Mavrodi had established "Stock Generation", a pyramid scheme under the guise of a virtual stock exchange, registered in the Caribbean. Despite a warning on the website, thousands lost money. It was shut down by the US Securities and Exchange Commission in 2000.

MMM-2011 was another scheme of Russia's Bernie Madoff. Launched in 2011 as an online venture, Mavrodi said his intention was to disrupt the unfair global financial system.

There were no investments in securities or anything forming part of the financial world; individual investors could send money to other investors and also receive money. Mavrodi said it was a "community of ordinary people selflessly helping each other".

He wrote to Julian Assange looking to cooperate on his new operation to fight "against the hypocritical global financial clique", which was, in reality, a Ponzi scheme coupled with a pyramid scheme. New investors funded earlier investors and received commissions in the form of Bitcoin when they introduced new members.

This new MMM went global when Mavrodi started new ventures in South America, Africa and Asia. Those putting money in were promised a return of 20 per cent a month for ordinary investors – 30 per cent for pensioners. Just as in Russia, while some made money, most were financially ruined.

Mavrodi died in 2018 after a heart attack. He was 62. Despite this, MMM schemes continue to operate in countries around the world.

An earlier advertising slogan stated, "There are no problems at MMM."

CHAMOY OPERATION

You can earn a place in the history books by being the first to step on a planetary body or by inventing a type of computer. Chamoy Thipyaso gained her place in history by being given the longest-ever prison sentence: 141,078 years for fraud.

In the mid-1970s, she set up a "chit fund". Used in India and other Asian countries, a chit fund is a financial arrangement whereby investors pay in a certain amount each month with the guarantee of a monthly return and a large payment at some point during the lifetime of the fund. The organizer takes a fee.

Thipyaso's chit fund – the Mae Chamoy Fund – was said to be invested in oil shipments, which were supposed to offer high returns on investment. An investor could double their money in 16 months. Over 17,000 people invested about eight billion Thai bahts, equivalent to around $300 million. Included in the group of investors were members of the Thai royal family. Over 70 per cent of investors were military personnel. To gain entry, investors had to be introduced by existing members.

Chamoy Thipyaso's husband was an officer in the Royal Thai Air Force. She had no business background and had worked as a hairdresser and a government clerk for the Thai

Petroleum Authority. Their connections to the petroleum industry and the military – a powerful element in Thai society – coupled with prestigious investors lent the scheme a great level of credibility and encouraged further subscribers.

As well as voluntarily paying in money, those in the military were pressured to invest. A further "incentive": investors were threatened with being barred from investing again if they withdrew their money. Members were promised a return of 6.5 per cent a month, a fantastic return and one to tempt the most cautious of investors. As the military was connected, and thousands had already put in money, surely investors' money was as safe as houses?

However, in the 1980s, it was discovered that she had taken millions of dollars from those who had trusted her. Fear spread in 1984 that investors' money might be lost. At one point, Thipyaso had to meet a crowd of worried clients who'd gathered at her lavish suburban home. She proclaimed through a loudhailer that they would all get their money back.

In March 1985, she failed to make an interest payment, the first time this had happened in the ten-year-long running of the fund. Even when it looked like existing investors might not get their money back, new investors ploughed money in – some of them remortgaging their houses.

Thipyaso then disappeared, with an estimated 400 million baht. In her trademark large sunglasses, she reappeared in June, telling investors they wouldn't receive all their money back after all. That month, she was arrested and charged with fraud. It followed a single complaint, which was swiftly followed by hundreds more.

It was thought the initial complaint came from a group of younger Air Force and Army officers who had joined the money pool more recently and who had most to lose, the classic result of a Ponzi scheme when the money runs out. They had found out that Thipyaso could only pay them back 3 per cent of what was owed.

The first person to complain to the police had lost 160,000 baht ($5,800), but others lost much more. One Air Force officer lost 81 million baht ($3 million). Military leaders urged those who had lost money to take legal action to recover their money. It was thought that the losses of the royal family and senior military figures were made good when Thipyaso disappeared and before others were alerted.

After her arrest, Thipyaso promised to pay back investors a portion of their outlay without saying how much. She then claimed her agents had cheated her, and she had hardly any money left. By July, government officials estimated that four billion baht ($145 million) that had been resting in Thipyaso's account had been transferred to VIPs, family and the agents involved in the running of the scheme.

In 1984, worry about their effect on the country's finances if they failed led to chit funds, or "high-yielding pyramid money games" as they were described in the media at the time, being made illegal in Thailand by royal decree. Despite this, Thipyaso continued operating and investors, desperate not to miss out on a source of income that had worked well for others, kept giving her their money.

While in jail in Bangkok, Thipyaso was kept under close guard to both prevent any suicide attempt and to protect her from any attempted attack on her life. Along with seven others involved in the running of the scheme, she was put on trial in 1989. When found guilty of corporate fraud, it was then that she was given her world record sentence.

Ultimately, she only spent 0.006 per cent of her sentence behind bars, being released after eight years. Thai law at the time prevented anyone found guilty of fraud from spending more than 20 years in jail. Despite her shorter term in prison, her sentence still stands as a world record.

Others have also received incredible sentences for financial crimes. In 2017, Thai fraudster Pudit Kittithradilok was given 13,275 years of jail time for a Ponzi and pyramid scheme that took in $160 million from 40,000 investors who were told they'd earn more if they recruited other investors. Kittithradilok's sentence was halved since he confessed, so he only faced 6,637 years. Faruk Fatih Ozer from Turkey was given 11,196 years in 2023 for taking $43 million from 2,000 customers through the cryptocurrency exchange Thodex. And in 2012, Mexican man José Luis González was sentenced to 2,035 years for fraud involving taking down payments for motor vehicles which were never delivered.

REED ALL ABOUT IT

A Ponzi scheme stands out when it is associated with celebrity and religion. American man Reed Slatkin developed such a scheme with what was, at the time, one of the biggest investment frauds in US financial history.

Slatkin was born in 1949 and, as a teenager, became a Scientologist. His uncle had introduced him to the church after Slatkin's father had died, and it served as a source of comfort for the grieving youngster.

Scientology is recognized as a religion in some countries, including the US. In Scientology, humans have immortal souls called "thetans" that go through different lifetimes accruing traumas, which can be "audited" out so the souls become "clear". The first churches of Scientology were founded in the 1950s by science fiction writer L. Ron Hubbard. Slatkin studied with Hubbard and, in 1975, became an ordained minister.

In 1986, Slatkin started acting as a full-time investment adviser to fellow Scientologists. He promised annual returns of around 24 per cent a year for investors and would take 10 per cent of the profits as his fee.

Living in Hope Ranch, an affluent suburb of Santa Barbara in California, he had a ready supply of rich investors. Those who gave him their money included Hollywood movie actors and executives such as actors Anne Archer, Giovanni Ribisi, Joe Pantoliano and *Fight Club* producer Art Linson.

Showing the level of his connections in Tinseltown, for Slatkin's 50th birthday, movie stars Kevin Costner and Arnold Schwarzenegger sent video messages.

Other investors were tech entrepreneurs, wealthy people he knew through living in Santa Barbara, and fellow Scientologists. As part of this exclusive community, he was able to encourage investments through social engagements. Slatkin used a tactic often used by the grafter: make the scheme exclusive and difficult to get into, thus making it, to those seeing profits being made by others, that much more attractive.

Returns for the "Reed Slatkin Investment Club" were supposed to have come from trading stocks. Investors were under the impression he started working at 5 a.m. to time with the opening of stock exchanges on the East Coast in New York. To beat his competitors, he used complicated computer programmes he'd devised to trade. His "war room" was a converted garage.

Slatkin did invest in various companies, but they weren't too successful and didn't produce much in the way of returns. One was a theme park never built. As in any good old-fashioned Ponzi scheme, it didn't matter as the early investors received their expected high returns from those joining later.

Slatkin's share provided him with plenty of money to indulge his taste for art, aircraft (he owned two) and automobiles. He also purchased properties in Oregon and New Mexico.

In 1994, he struck gold when he invested money in a venture created by an entrepreneur called Sky Dayton, who had an idea to build an internet service provider company.

Slatkin was introduced to Dayton by fellow Scientologist Kevin O'Donnell. The online world was about to produce big rewards for those getting in at the start; the resulting company, EarthLink was a huge success.

In 1999, Slatkin was investigated by the financial authorities for being an unregistered investment adviser, but he continued taking in money. In May 2001, the Securities and Exchange Commission obtained a restraining order and froze Slatkin's assets. Investigations continued, and he was arrested in April 2002. After collaborating with the investigators, he pleaded guilty to 15 charges of mail and wire fraud, conspiracy to obstruct justice and money laundering.

In September 2003, Slatkin was given a jail sentence of 14 years, one fewer than the duration of the scam. When being sentenced, he expressed regret for betraying the trust of all the investors, saying he was left "detesting my conduct and detesting myself".

He was also ordered to repay $240 million that had been lost by investors. Eight hundred people had invested a total of $593 million – and around 75 had made huge profits. Although some had made profits, many more had lost their life savings, children's college funds or their retirement incomes.

Some missed out on medical treatments by giving Slatkin's club all their money. One investor described him as the "Ted Bundy of the financial world". Another, whose terminally ill father gave Slatkin $7.3 million, said he was a great white shark, preying on "the sick, the dying, the young, the innocent and the vulnerable".

At his sentencing, Slatkin had claimed there was pressure from other Scientologists to keep the scam continuing so they would continue to profit. Many of his investors had put some of their profits into the church. Slatkin said he had fears for his family if he stopped. The judge in his case found little evidence of direct pressure on him.

Two associates of Slatkin were also jailed. Richard D. McMullin was given five months' jail time, and fellow Scientologist Daniel W. Jacobs was given four for helping Slatkin delay an investigation by the Securities and Exchange Commission. Documents were faked showing the supposed investments in a fictional Swiss brokerage firm. Jacobs pretended to be a representative of the European-based firm.

Slatkin was released from prison in 2013 but died of a heart attack two years later. He had been excommunicated from the Scientologists in 2001.

PUMPED AND DUMPED

Several scammers and swindlers have had their lives portrayed on screen. A smaller number are those whose lives were depicted in memoirs they wrote while in prison.

One of these is Jordan Belfort, who wrote *The Wolf of Wall Street* (and *Catching the Wolf of Wall Street*) while in the Taft Correctional Institution in California.

The books depict a life of excess. In the offices of the company Belfort founded, employees enjoyed the company of sex workers, drug dealers and exotic animals. Belfort took copious amounts of drugs and alcohol. He bought a yacht once owned by Coco Chanel and watched it sink after ordering the captain to steer it towards a storm. He almost crashed a helicopter while attempting to land while stoned. He commuted to work in a white Ferrari Testarossa sports car, just like the one driven by Don Johnson in TV cop show *Miami Vice*.

The hedonistic lifestyle was paid for by the takings of his brokerage firm, Stratton Oakmont, founded by Belfort and Danny Porush in 1989. The Long Island-based company wasn't a Wall Street firm. Instead it operated by buying and selling shares "over the counter", i.e. away from stock exchanges.

What had put Belfort inside?

Belfort was in prison for fraud, for committing what is known as "pump-and-dump" schemes. These are when false statements are made about a company in order to boost its share price. As the price goes up, at the right moment, shares are sold by the trader behind the ploy, who bought them when they were cheaper. These traders tend to have a large number of shares, and when these are sold, the price drops. Those other shareholders who haven't sold at the right time, or who hang onto them, lose out when the price drops below what they bought.

Stratton Oakmont became a very successful company taking in millions, but it started small. Belfort had worked on Wall Street for investment firm L. F. Rothschild but lost his job after the Black Monday stock market crash of 1987. He began working at a small "boiler room" company selling penny stocks – those worth less than a dollar each. Showing his sales skills, Belfort quickly started earning enough to set up on his own with business partner Danny Porush. They used a friend's former car showroom as premises.

Belfort didn't employ experienced stockbrokers; instead, he hired people he could train up to follow his sales techniques. At one point, a thousand traders were working for Stratton Oakmont. It was one of the biggest over-the-counter firms in the US.

However, the company's operations were always under observation by the authorities, and by 1996, they had amassed enough evidence to ban it from selling or buying shares. Stratton Oakmont went out of business.

Three years later, Belfort and Porush were both charged with securities fraud and money laundering. Belfort was given four years in prison and served 22 months after agreeing a plea bargain with the FBI. His partner spent 39 months in jail.

An estimated 1,500 investors lost $200 million, and Belfort was ordered to pay back just over half this amount. Half of his future earnings were assigned to paying off this debt. He received more than $2 million for the book and film rights to his story. Belfort's prison-written memoirs were made into a movie directed by famed Hollywood director Martin Scorsese and starring Leonardo DiCaprio as Belfort. It was released in 2013.

OUT OF ENERGY

Shareholders and those with a financial interest in a company rely on those in charge being transparent and trustworthy. The giant US energy conglomerate Enron collapsed in 2001 when the very opposite of this took place.

Enron was founded in 1985 after a merger of two energy companies, Houston Natural Gas and InterNorth. Kenneth Lay, who was CEO of Houston Natural Gas, became the overall CEO and chairman of the new company. It provided natural gas and went on to be involved in water treatment and broadband networks, as well as energy trading following the deregulation of the energy markets.

Jeffrey Skilling joined Enron in 1990. He pursued an aggressive strategy to grow the company. One of the methods was mark-to-market accounting, where assets are valued as to what their current market value is perceived to be rather than the book value. Projected profits can be listed as actual profits. The decision as to what was put down on the balance sheet was in the hands of the company's management. Enron did this when it entered into a partnership with video rental company Blockbuster to provide video on demand.

By 2000, Enron was worth $68 billion. In February 2001, Skilling was appointed CEO and, after Lay stepped aside, became chairman. Enron employees were given unrealistic targets for company earnings by management based on expectations set by analysts and not on what was reasonably achievable. When the actual results didn't match, such as the Blockbuster deal, creative accountancy was used to cover them up.

In August 2001, Lay received a letter from vice-president Sherron Watkins outlining the fraudulent practices going on in the company. Enron was using complicated practices to hide its failings. One method was "special purpose entities". These were shell companies where large amounts of debt and bad assets could be hidden, out of sight of investors and anyone else interested in the performance of the company. The shell companies were hiding Enron's losses while, to the outside world, the company was growing and still worthy of an investment-grade credit rating.

The company's share price had gone from $30 a share in 1998 to rise to $90 in the middle of 2001. This rise did not go unnoticed. Speculation started circulating as no one could quite understand how Enron made its money. The SEC started investigating what was eventually found to be one of the largest corporate frauds for a US company.

Skilling did not stay as CEO of the company for long, departing in August 2001 (just six months after he took the position). He could see the writing on the wall and cashed in $60 million of shares. Lay also sold millions of dollars worth of Enron stock; he made a profit of $217 million.

Lay resumed the position of CEO and faced losses in every department of the company. Company assets had been overvalued by billions of dollars. For example, a Brazilian power plant had been overvalued by a billion dollars.

He considered several options, such as restructuring, a merger and even selling off Enron's crucial pipelines. Lay discussed with the senior management team the financial problems – there were losses of at least $7 billion in the company's assets and business units.

In October 2001, Enron announced losses of $1 billion. Lay tried to allay fears, saying they were non-recurring, i.e. a one-off event. However, the crisis was not going away. By November, the share price had fallen to $0.26 and in December, Enron filed for Chapter 11 – it was bankrupt. At the time, it was the largest company bankruptcy in US history. Twenty thousand employees lost their jobs. They also lost their pensions.

For overseeing Enron's corporate misconduct, Lay and Skilling faced charges and were tried together. Defence lawyers claimed they were not aware of what was going on and laid the blame at the door of Enron's chief financial officer, Andrew Fastow. Fastow pleaded guilty to charges of wire and securities fraud and cooperated with the authorities in the cases against other Enron employees. He was sentenced to six years in jail.

In May 2006, Lay and Skilling were convicted on fraud, conspiracy and insider trading charges. Lay did not serve any time, as he died before sentencing. Skilling received 24 years in jail and was fined $45 million. He was released in 2019 after spending 12 years behind bars.

The scandal also had wider effects. Enron's accounting firm, Arthur Andersen – one of the Big Five accountancy firms alongside EY, KPMG, Deloitte and PwC – was found to have behaved criminally: obstructing justice by shredding documents pertaining to the company. It lost its audit licence and went out of business. Legislative changes were introduced to prevent similar behaviour in the future.

When Lay and Skilling were indicted, Deputy Attorney General James Comey said they (and others) "oversaw a massive conspiracy to cook the books at Enron and to create the illusion that it was a robust, growing company with limitless potential when, in fact, Enron was an increasingly troubled business kept afloat only by a series of deceptions".

SWINDLERS

While some con artists fall more easily into certain categories, there are some who are just out-and-out swindlers. Their cons can be complicated or very simple, but their aims are generally straightforward: to make money at the expense of others.

They can take many forms. There are the television cheats who were provided with the answers to quiz questions or those who enlisted help so the show would cough up the prize money. "Canoe Man" John Darwin conjured up a scheme to resolve his debts through a life insurance scam, and Italian telesales queen Wanna Marchi offered life-changing lottery numbers from a Brazilian psychic.

One of the greatest con artists who ever persuaded a victim to part with their money told everyone that a country's fortunes rested on giving him their money so that he could get them a tenfold return on their investment, a great long con that lasted two decades. Another who exhibited perhaps the biggest amount of brazen cheek was the American who used stolen credit cards to order goods and services from his prison cell.

While we can condemn their crimes and the heartbreak the financial losses can cause, we can admit to some level of admiration for the sheer gall exhibited by those who have epitomized the word "swindler".

UP THE CREEK WITHOUT A PADDLE

Many people who move to sunnier climes do so after winning lotteries or through a lifetime of hard work providing a decent pension. Few do so after canoeing off the north east coast of England and faking their own death. This is what Durham-born John Darwin did in 2002.

Darwin was 51 years old when he decided to fake his own passing. He had been a teacher and was working as a prison officer, but in 2002 had run into debt following the purchase of two houses. Darwin and his wife Anne ran a business renting out bedsit properties, but customers weren't as plentiful as they needed.

Fearing bankruptcy, Darwin had pondered the idea of faking his death in order to receive a payout of life insurance money. The idea was put into action on 21 March 2002. On a calm day, Darwin got into his canoe and paddled out from his coastal hometown of Seaton Carew into the North Sea.

Or at least that was his hope. Darwin was reported missing when he didn't turn up for work at Holme House Prison. A search involving lifeboats and a Royal Air Force search and rescue helicopter was carried, out but didn't find him.

A paddle and the wreckage of his canoe were eventually found on the shore.

Despite no body being found, Darwin was declared dead a year later, and, with the death certificate, Anne could claim the insurance money, which came in at £250,000.

But where was Darwin?

He was at home. After paddling out from Seaton Carew, he'd headed south and landed near to North Gare pier, a mile down the coast from his house. Once ashore, Darwin pushed his canoe back into the sea. He'd then phoned his wife at her work and arranged to be collected from a car park. He was taken to Durham railway station, where he set off to lie low until interest subsided. After a few weeks of camping in the Lake District, he came home. When visitors came – including John and Anne's sons – Darwin would squeeze through a secret passageway hidden behind a wardrobe into a bedsit next door. Their two sons, Mark and Anthony, were not told of their father's survival.

Darwin was almost caught several times despite growing his hair and a beard. Once, when a resident of one of his bedsits recognized him, Darwin was able to prevent being revealed by asking him to say nothing. Another time, he was spotted gardening by a colleague.

Looking for a place in the sun, the Darwins considered moving to the Mediterranean island of Cyprus. The obstacle of John being dead was overcome by his applying for a passport in the name of someone else. He chose "John Jones", the name of a baby who had died in 1950 – the same year Darwin was born. The passport was issued in 2004, and this allowed him to leave the UK to visit Cyprus, the US, Gibraltar and Spain before the couple decided to move to Central America.

Arriving in July 2006, the Darwins met with a property agent in Panama. A photograph was taken by the agent and posted online. They returned in March 2007 to purchase an apartment in El Dorado in Panama City and then two months later bought an estate near the Panama Canal where they hoped to build a hotel. In October 2007, their home in Seaton Carew was sold for £300,000, and the money transferred to Panama. Anne followed soon after.

Before moving abroad, when Anne was working as a receptionist at a medical centre, their plan began to unravel. A colleague overheard Anne's whispered phone conversations and suspected who she was talking to. The police were contacted in September 2007 and began their investigations. When the photo of the Darwins and the property agent in Panama came to light, it was proof that Anne was not a widow as claimed and John was alive and well.

In Panama, John Darwin faced an insurmountable obstacle. In order to invest in the country, he would need a visa, and as a UK national, the police in Britain would have to be contacted. His John Jones persona would not stand up to any rigorous inspection, so he decided on another plan.

On 1 December 2007, Darwin entered a police station in London and said he was John Darwin and that he had no memory from the past five years. He said, "I think I may be a missing person." Still in Panama, Anne was said to be delighted at the return of her husband, who had been missing all those years. Her sons were also delighted, but this was soon replaced by anger when they discovered they had been duped by their parents for five years. They said they never wanted to speak with their parents again. John's father, Ronald, cut him out of his will. He died in 2012, feeling betrayed by his son.

The police investigations resulted in both Darwins appearing in court on fraud charges. Both were found guilty. In July 2008, John received a sentence of six years, three months in prison, and Anne got three months longer. They were released on parole three years later.

The two had received over half a million pounds in insurance and pension money. The money was recovered through the sale of their Panamanian properties. It left them with no assets.

John and Anne divorced. John married a woman in the Philippines; Anne wrote a memoir of the events entitled *Out of My Depth*. She claimed that she'd only gone along with the scheme because her ex-husband was very persuasive and said that it was only to last a short time.

The story of the "canoe man" and his disappearance caught the public's imagination and inspired several TV dramas and comedies. There was a certain amount of fun to be had over what was a serious crime.

The hotel situated close to the Darwin's home renamed its restaurant the "Darwin Room". In Seaton Carew, when the deception was revealed, some pranksters erected a sign in the town, "Welcome to Seaton Canoe – Twinned with Panama".

QUIZ SHOW CHEATS

Television game shows offer a combination of fame, excitement and the chance of a cash prize or other valuable rewards. At times, the temptation to gain an unfair advantage can be too enticing and a way of cheating is looked for. One famous example saw a contestant cheating but with the added element of the show's producers being in on the act.

American game show *Twenty-One* gave contestants the chance to win big money prizes. They had to answer individual questions on general knowledge while standing in a booth, unable to hear the other contestant's answers. The first to get 21 points was the winner of a round, and five rounds made up a show. Cash prizes would be paid out, the amount depending on how much of a points difference there was between the two competitors.

On 28 November 1956, college professor Charles Van Doren made his first appearance. He came from a literary family: his father was a Pulitzer Prize-winning poet, and his mother a novelist and editor. The 31-year-old Van Doren taught English at New York's Columbia University.

Van Doren had been approached by one of the show's producers, Al Freedman. The current long-running champion was Herb Stempel, who was in the middle of a six-week-long run of wins. The winner stayed on the show until they lost. Those behind the show, including presenter Jack Barry, thought someone new was needed, as the show was losing viewers.

The urbane Van Doren would provide a contrast with the ill-dressed, working-class Stempel. The competitors drew the first two shows. Ratings grew as viewers tuned in to see if challenger Van Doren could beat the champion Stempel. This he did on 5 December 1956 in front of an estimated 50 million viewers. Could he continue his winning streak? Yes. For 14 weeks, until losing to Vivienne Nearing on 11 March. Van Doren amassed a prize total of $128,000 – a lot of money now and a larger amount then.

But all was not as it seemed. It turned out that Van Doren had been coached since the start by the show's producers, Dan Enright and Al Freedman. He was shown how to build up tension before answering and, more importantly, was shown the questions he'd face. Not only that but Stempel had also been given the questions before each show.

Following his successful television appearances, Van Doren was given a lucrative three-year contract and appeared on several programmes, including *The Today Show*.

Stempel was unhappy with his treatment. He'd not received the money he was due and, in order to get some of it, signed a document saying that he hadn't been coached on his answers. A promise of an appearance on another game show had not been kept. Stempel had talked to journalists about how these high-profile shows were fixed, but his whistleblowing wasn't taken seriously. Then, in May 1958, it was reported that another TV game show, *Dotto*, on CBS, was rigged. Stempel's claims were published; NBC denied any wrongdoing had taken place. The story wasn't going away.

In 1958, Van Doren was questioned by Joseph Stone, Manhattan's assistant district attorney, but lied, saying he was not given the quiz show's answers. He also maintained his position to a grand jury. A year later, during a congressional investigation into TV quiz show fixing, Van Doren admitted he had, in fact, been involved in the fixing of the shows, saying, "I have deceived my friends, and I had millions of them."

Van Doren was charged with committing perjury at the grand jury and was found guilty, being given a suspended prison sentence. NBC fired him, and he resigned from his academic post at Columbia. He put his general knowledge to work, becoming editor-in-chief of the *Encyclopaedia Britannica*. None of the show's producers faced criminal charges as no crime had been committed. Presenter Jack Barry's career suffered a dip, but he eventually returned to prime time with game show *The Joker's Wild*.

*

Across the Atlantic, a British contestant also required assistance to win big.

In 2001, Charles Ingram was a British Army major who had served in Bosnia. In September of that year, he appeared on ITV game show *Who Wants to Be a Millionaire?*

The show has a simple format: individual contestants are asked 15 general knowledge questions and pick their answers from four offered. The contestant accrues winnings after every question answered correctly. If they answer all 15 questions correctly, they win a million pounds. The player has assistance through lifelines: by being able to phone a friend to see if they know the answer, have half the answers removed from a question, and ask the audience to vote on what they think is the correct answer. A contestant can choose to leave the game at any time if they wish to take their accrued winnings. They are guaranteed certain "milestone" cash amounts as they move up the ladder of prizes, which roughly double each rung. The maximum safety net is £32,000.

To get the chance to sit in the hot seat to answer the questions, potential contestants have to be the quickest in answering a question that involves placing four items in order. The "Fastest Finger First" test is done electronically. In the weeks before appearing on the show, Ingram used a homemade machine to practise.

Ingram's wife Diana and her brother Adrian had both been on the show, winning £32,000 each, but Ingram wanted to do better. His preparations worked, and he made it through "Fastest Finger First" and took his place in the hot seat opposite question master Chris Tarrant.

Ingram got the first set of questions correct without using any lifelines. But on question six, about British TV soap opera *Coronation Street* for £2,000, he used the "Ask the Audience" lifeline. On the next question, for £4,000, he had to "Phone a Friend" to get the right response. The day's play ended. The programme's staff thought that having used two lifelines, Ingram would not be in the show much longer.

Ingram returned the next day to complete his game. He said he would not be so conservative. He got through the £8,000 and £16,000 questions but faced difficulty on the £32,000 one. Ingram took the "50:50" option and was left with two possible answers to which musical artist released an album called *Born to Do It* in 2000. When he aired his thoughts on which was the right answer – pop band A1 – the audience's startled reaction resulted in him changing his mind... and getting it correct with his answer, Craig David.

For £64,000, he stated the answer early in his deliberations over what sport had a match called "gentlemen versus players". Cricket was the correct response. Another right answer came for £125,000 over a question on which artist painted *The Ambassadors*: Holbein. For a quarter of a million pounds, he had to know what kind of garment an "Anthony Eden" was. He said "hat", which was correct.

With the stakes incredibly high, he played for £500,000. To win, he had to know which city Baron Haussmann designed. Ingram talked through the four possibilities of Athens, Berlin, Paris or Rome. He seemed to favour Berlin but then stuck with Paris – and won.

For the top prize of one million pounds, Ingram faced the question of what was the name for a number one followed by a hundred zeros. If Ingram chose wrongly, he'd lose £468,000. After admitting he'd never heard of it, he chose "googol". And won.

Among the celebrations, Ingram's wife Diana joined him on the set and said, "How the hell did you do it?"

It turned out that he hadn't done it on his own. Following Ingram's stuttering first day's performance, they recruited a fellow contestant, Tecwen Whittock. The plan was simple: when Ingram talked through the potential answers, Whittock would cough to indicate the correct one.

The plan worked. However, the celebrations were to be short-lived as a member of the production team alerted the producers that there were irregularities: it was alleged that coughing on the set coincided with Ingram deliberating over the answers. The cheque for £1 million was retained by the show's producers.

The police were called, and Charles and Diana Ingram and Tecwen Whittock faced charges of "procuring the execution of a valuable security by deception". The valuable security being the cheque for a million pounds.

In 2003, after a four-week trial, the jury found them guilty by a majority verdict. All were given suspended prison sentences and fined. The Ingrams were ordered to pay the defence costs. It all added up to over a hundred thousand pounds.

Charles Ingram maintained his innocence and was backed in his claims by writer and investigator Jon Ronson. Tecwen Whittock claimed he had a persistent cough and couldn't help coughing during the show's recording. Ronson spoke with another contestant who said that coughing from the audience happened all the time.

Whatever the truth, Ingram did not profit from his appearance on the show. He and his wife have declared themselves bankrupt four times since 2001.

WANNA MAKE MONEY

Television shopping channels first appeared in the late 1970s. The format was the same wherever broadcast: presenters would demonstrate the goods on sale, and interested viewers could telephone to place an order. Two of the most successful presenters sold their wares in Italy, but their sales techniques landed them in court.

Vanna Marchi was born in 1942 in Bologna but used the name Wanna. She was married in 1961, but on her wedding day, her mother-in-law called her "ugly" – to her face – something that affected her deeply. Her husband, Raimondo Nobile, was a drinks salesman. They had two children together: a son, Maurizio (born in 1961), and a daughter, Stefania (born in 1964).

Nobile had affairs and brought little in the way of money home. With the children growing up, Wanna went out to work and found employment as a beautician in a morgue. On one occasion, her talents were so good when working on a deceased daughter that the grieving mother gave her 1.5 million lire (worth around $1,800 then). Wanna bought a Fiat car with some of the money.

Wanna opened her own shop, selling perfume and beauty treatments. She knew the value of advertising and promoted her business on the radio. This brought more business, and she opened bigger premises.

In 1978, Wanna started selling on TV. Her first product was slimming cream, but her first couple of appearances on TV didn't sell any. When she started crying on screen, admitting that she wouldn't be coming back as she wasn't able to sell anything, the switchboards lit up with callers.

The slimming and anti-wrinkle creams sold well, but her biggest seller was a slimming alga. Her sales technique was confrontational, directly insulting potential clients. She shouted at them, calling them "fat" or "hairy" or blamed them for putting on weight after getting married. Those who turned down the offer to buy a product were called "idiots" by this "tele-barker" (a derogatory term for those "tele marketers" who were aggressive on air). Her catchphrase was yelling "*D'accordo?!*" (Okay?!) at viewers.

Wanna's daughter Stefania started selling on TV when aged 15. She sold anti-cellulite products. A huge seller for the Marchi mum and daughter sales team was the "Belly Melter" – a unique slimming cream product that sold for years after its introduction in 1986.

They became wealthy celebrities, appearing on other TV shows and in 1989, Wanna released a pop song called "*D'accordo?!*". However, things were not going well in all areas of her life, as Wanna's marriage ended when Raimondo Nobile was kicked out. The couple had led different lives for several years. The "Queen of Television" also suffered a setback in 1986 when her shop was burned out. There were allegations of Mafia involvement in the fire-starting and also in extortion attempts that came afterwards. Wanna received phone calls asking for over a billion lire (over seven hundred thousand dollars). A wheelchair with Stefania's name on it was left outside their villa. This extortion was stopped due to the intervention of other shadowy figures in the criminal underworld.

In 1988, Wanna met Francesco Campana, who worked in IT. They sold their rights to a magazine for a double wedding with Stefania in Miami. It was a sham, as Wanna was not divorced.

In 1989, Wanna brought out a new product: a perfume called Flag. It wasn't a success, and soon the company couldn't pay its bills: revenue didn't meet the outgoings; they'd spent a lot on marketing the perfume. Wanna's company went bankrupt in March 1990 with a deficit of figures stated from 1.2 to four billion lire ($900,000 – $3 million) There were allegations the bankruptcy trustee was then attacked, through Wanna's connections with the Mafia. Wanna and Stefania were arrested and charged with fraudulent bankruptcy. They received short jail sentences.

In 1994, Wanna started up in business again, backed by the charming, self-styled Marquis Attilio Capra de Carrè. On TV, Wanna and Stefania were joined by Brazilian "psychic", Mario Do Nascimento. He brought a sense of the mysterious supernatural with him, based on his ancestry: his grandmother was a priestess in the Candomblé religion, which is an amalgamation of Catholicism and African belief systems. Do Nascimento was known on TV as "The Master of Life".

Business was good, and they became the top telesales operation in Italy, but in 1996, Wanna, Stefania and Do Nascimento split from the Marquis to set up their own company, Asciè.

With slimming creams and algae not providing as rich a vein of income as before, a new income stream was launched: magic. The Master of Life provided "personalized" horoscopes and "lucky" lottery numbers to be bought for 80,000 lire each. If buyers hadn't won money and phoned the company, they would be told that there was something negative in their lives, a jinx, or the "evil eye" that was preventing their good fortune. If they purchased a card reading or an amulet from The Master, then their luck would change.

Another product rolled out was "Holy Salt". The buyer would receive a parcel of salt, which they'd have to put in a glass of water and then store in a cupboard for a week, alongside their lottery numbers. When these numbers were played – a win was guaranteed. If no win occurred, then they'd have to buy another product to cleanse the negativity away.

Customers could be phoned up years after buying a product. The sales operators would harass them to buy further items. If they refused, they could be told that a relative was in potential danger. The emotional pressure resulted in many customers spending more money than they could afford. One mother spent 200 million lire. Marriages broke apart under the strain of financial pressures caused by overspending on Asciè products.

In November 2001, an investigative news programme, *Striscia la Notizia*, broadcast footage of a customer turning down the offer of buying further "good luck" items. Stefania came on the call and said she'd call the police on her and told the customer she'd never sleep again. It provoked investigations by the police. The Marquis was suspected of giving them information as he had been unhappy when Wanna and Stefania set up their own company without him.

SWINDLERS

The police found that between 1996 and 2002, Asciè made profits of 61 billion lire. The database of customers numbered over 300,000. Most victims were vulnerable women easily persuaded to hand over money.

Wanna, Stefania, Do Nascimento, and Wanna's partner, Francesco Campana, were charged with various offences. Do Nascimento went back to Brazil and avoided jail time. Campana was eventually pardoned. Wanna and Stefania were sentenced to ten years in prison for criminal conspiracy and fraud. They had to recompense their victims. They served six years and were released for good behaviour.

WEISS SQUAD

Sholam Weiss was born in 1954 and grew up in New York. He started working while young, being a delivery boy for his father's fruit stand. In 1974, he bought a plumbing company, Windsor Plumbing Supply, and built it up to a $20 million business before it went bankrupt in the 1980s. Weiss had used some of his money to be a part-owner of New York's legendary nightclub Studio 54.

In 1994, Weiss spent eight months in prison on mail fraud changes for a false insurance claim stemming from a 1986 warehouse fire that he claimed had destroyed a million dollars worth of bathtubs. However, a far larger sentence was to result from his involvement in another insurance company.

The National Heritage Life Insurance Company was based in Orlando, Florida, but had been performing badly. In 1989, falling sales of its single premium policies saw its overall revenues decline by 34 per cent. The company's poor financial state meant that in May 1990, the Delaware Insurance Commissioner, Donna Lee Williams, stepped in and instructed National Heritage to raise capital to provide a sufficient surplus. If it didn't, the company could be shut down. (Williams had jurisdiction as National Heritage was registered in Delaware.)

National Heritage and its parent company, Lifeco Investment Group, were then sold. The new owner was an investment group called Tri-Atlantic Holdings. It would provide $4 million to supply the needed capital and, in return, would gain a controlling interest. In June 1990, the proposal was agreed.

Tri-Atlantic's takeover bid was weak in one area: it did not have the necessary funds. To make the takeover payment, a series of complex transactions were carried out by one of Tri-Atlantic's directors, David Davies, an Orlando accountant, and Michael Blutrich, a New York lawyer with connections to the Gambino crime family. These labyrinthine moves resulted in National Heritage's own money being used for its acquisition. The company's assets were reduced by $3 million during the process.

Those now in control of National Heritage then started a programme of keeping the company going in order to take money from it. Real estate was used. In one instance, a loan was granted to buy a horse farm. The farm cost half a million dollars, but the loan, which appeared as an asset on the company's books, was for $2.5 million. The surplus two million dollars went to an account controlled by one of the directors, Patrick Smythe, a businessman from Arizona.

One purchase for land in New York state cost $1 million, but five million had been taken from the company to pay for it. The owners pocketed the surplus. The list went on. An amusement park in the Catskills was recorded in the accounts as being ten times more valuable than its real worth. The company invested in a New York strip club and paid protection money to the Gambino crime family. This connection brought interest from the FBI, who raided the club and subsequently charged the Gambino family's boss, John Gotti Jr, with extortion.

In 1994, the Delaware Insurance Department began an examination of the company. When examiners asked for corroborating evidence of the loan-securing collateral, nothing was produced. In May 1994, Williams placed the company in receivership; it was liquidated the following year. Lawyers were hired to try to retrieve lost assets.

When a tip-off was sent to the US Attorney's Office about suspect loans, the federal authorities began their own investigations. The FBI and Internal Revenue Service got involved. These organizations would spend five years trying to piece together what had happened. It was no easy task – those involved in National Heritage had been expert at forging paperwork and covering their tracks.

Sholam Weiss first became involved in the company in 1993 when asked by Michael Blutrich to try to sort out the company's finances. He was given $100 million to buy up mortgages that they could present on the company's accounts as being worth $135 million. He spent $65 million on mortgages that looked unlikely to be paid back; the rest he transferred to his own bank accounts in Israel and Switzerland.

The combined looting cost National Heritage hundreds of millions of dollars. The money disappearing meant that thousands of the insurer's 25,000 customers lost their life savings. But $420 million was eventually paid to policy and annuity holders from state guaranty funds and whatever money was left in the company.

Weiss was arrested, and after a nine-month trial, in November 1999, he was found guilty on 78 charges, including money laundering, racketeering, wire fraud and interstate transportation of stolen funds. Michael Blutrich testified against Weiss and entered the witness protection programme.

As the jury was deliberating their decision, Weiss fled. Rewards totalling $100,000 were posted for information leading to his capture. Weiss made the most of his time on the run, travelling to South America, then Europe and the Middle East. He spent large amounts of money staying in expensive hotels, gambling and hiring sex workers.

It was thought he had access to between $225 and $250 million of National Heritage money. In October 2000, a much slimmer and less hirsute Weiss was apprehended in Austria, but it took until May 2002 until "Charles Dick" – the name he had adopted – was extradited.

In his absence, Weiss had been given an 845-year jail sentence – the longest for a white-collar crime in the US (although this was later reduced to 835 years after appeal). He was also fined $123.4 million, ordered to pay National Heritage $125 million in restitution and to forfeit assets and properties totalling $57 million. FBI agent Joe Judge said, "Sholam Weiss was a crime tsunami."

He wasn't the only one to be found guilty – 15 others were convicted. One received a sentence constructed in the same way as Weiss's – the judge adding the sentences for each charge consecutively – leaving him facing 740 years in jail.

Weiss's jail sentence was commuted by President Donald Trump on his last day in office in January 2021. Instead of being in prison until 2738 CE, Weiss was released.

The collapse of National Heritage is thought to be the biggest failure of an insurance company brought down by fraud. It is estimated to have lost $450 million.

SCAMS AND SWINDLERS

Donna Lee Williams said, "You can make as many laws as you want, but there will always be that one individual who will try to cheat the system." Weiss was one of those individuals.

THE KAISER CHEATS

Many children dream of playing football professionally. However, to earn a living doing what they love is not achieved by all. Thousands fail to make the grade through injury, lack of opportunity or their own failings in skill, temperament or application.

The biggest football-loving country in the world is Brazil. The country's men's team has won the World Cup a record five times. They have a history of playing with a level of fluency, skill and flamboyance envied by many. Brazilian players are lauded as gods, existing on a different plane to their millions of fans. Some of the fans wish to take their relationship with these professional players a bit further than getting an autograph or a selfie. This aspect of being a footballer appealed to one unique man.

Carlos Kaiser – born Carlos Henrique Raposo in 1963 – signed for several professional football teams, including some of Brazil's biggest clubs. On the surface, this might look like a successful career in the game. The only trouble was that Carlos couldn't play. Nor did he want to.

Kaiser wanted to live the life of a top player without any of the activity on the pitch. He was fond of the party lifestyle and admitted that the time he spent in nightclubs meant he wasn't fit to train or play the next morning.

Kaiser had several elements in his modus operandi. He befriended top-level players such as Brazilian World Cup winners Carlos Alberto, Ricardo Rocha and Bebeto. Their recommendations would help him find new contacts at clubs prepared to sign him. He then ingratiated himself with the chairmen and presidents of the clubs so they would keep him on. In Mexico, he went out with the club president's niece, and this ploy helped keep him on their books for three years.

Once he arrived at a club, he said he lacked fitness and so spent his time working on physical work, avoiding touching a football, where his lack of talent would be immediate. When called upon to train with proper players and have to use the ball, he'd suddenly have an injury, such as a pulled hamstring or a ruptured tendon. MRI scans weren't available, so his ruse worked. He'd also pay other players to injure him during training. He once even asked a dentist to sign him off sick, somehow connecting leg problems with his teeth. If it looked like he was getting close to having to play, he would announce the death of his grandmother: she died at least four times.

He'd make himself useful to the other players, including providing women, so they'd ask club owners to retain him. He made contacts with journalists who could write fictional articles on his playing prowess. He used a toy mobile phone to have fake conversations with representatives of clubs (such as Barcelona) looking to sign him. When his fellow players found the toy phone in his kit bag, they just laughed it off. He was just Kaiser being Kaiser.

These tactics worked, and he signed for several professional clubs in Brazil, Mexico, the US, Argentina and France. In a country noted for its skilful exponents of the beautiful game, Kaiser ended up on the books of the Big Four clubs of Rio de Janeiro. In total, it is thought he signed for at least 11 clubs in a 26-year-long footballing career. Kaiser said later, "All the clubs I went to celebrated twice: when I signed and when I left."

At one point, he moved to Europe to sign for French side Gazélec Ajaccio, who played in Corsica. A potential banana skin arose when he was presented to the fans. To cover up his non-existent footballing skills, he kicked balls into the crowd while kissing the Corsican flag. When he returned to Brazil after a few months, a friendly journalist wrote a story portraying Kaiser as a successful goalscorer for the French club. However, things with Kaiser were not always crystal clear, and someone who played for Gazélec Ajaccio suggested Kaiser never signed for them but faked documentation and posed for photographs wearing a team strip he'd given him while still in Brazil.

When at Brazilian club Bangu, Kaiser was told to get stripped ready to go on as a substitute. The club's owner, crime boss Castor de Andrade, wanted to see Kaiser play. When his time came, rather than take to the field, the reluctant (and tired from partying) player jumped a fence and started fighting with the supporters, earning himself a red card despite not being on the pitch. Kaiser explained to an angry de Andrade that the fans were name-calling the club's owner, and he couldn't tolerate this, thinking of him as a father figure. De Andrade doubled his salary and extended his contract.

Kaiser's self-confidence and charm ensured he was not short of sexual partners. He claimed to have slept with a thousand women. One tactic to impress women was to claim to be an existing and successful player. He claimed to be Carlos Enrique, an Argentinean defender who won trophies while at

Talleres de Córdoba and Independiente. Other times, he said he was Brazilian international footballer Renata Gaúcho, as the two shared a physical resemblance. The two became friends, the friendship enduring even after the occasion when Gaúcho was refused admission to a nightclub because "he" was already there, enjoying the best table and chatting to beautiful women. The real Gaúcho, like many others, just laughed off Kaiser's cheek.

Kaiser's adopted surname came from the legendary German defender Franz Beckenbauer, whose dominant style earned him the nickname "The Kaiser" (The Emperor). That is where the similarities end. Beckenbauer played over 600 games, winning the World Cup twice. Carlos Kaiser won nothing but lasting infamy – and admiration from those impressed by his cheek and bravura. Renato Gaúcho called him "the greatest footballer never to play".

DRAKE'S PROGRESS

Francis Drake was a sixteenth-century naval explorer, famous for making the first circumnavigation of the world by an Englishman. He was also a privateer – someone given a free hand to act as a pirate. In his galleon *Golden Hind*, Drake attacked Spanish ports and ships. They called him "the Dragon" for his ruthless actions. Queen Elizabeth I kept over half the money brought back; Drake kept the rest and became a rich man.

Drake was knighted in 1581 for the treasure he'd supplied to the Crown's coffers. He had shown that England could rival Spain in maritime endeavours and even defeat its rival. Drake played a vital part in the defeat of the Spanish Armada in 1588, before which he was said to have insisted on finishing his game of bowls on Plymouth Hoe. Drake died in 1596. He had no children. Or did he?

As the years passed, a story gained ground that an heir able to inherit Drake's fortune had been found. They were descended from an illegitimate son, the result of an affair between the privateer and no less a person than Queen Elizabeth I! Money was needed to fund the heir's legal case to obtain their rightful money held by the British Crown. Many signed up on the promise of realizing a much larger return on their investment.

This inheritance scam had continued for centuries from the sixteenth century onwards in Britain. By the nineteenth century, it had crossed the Atlantic. At the start of the twentieth century, fraudsters looked through telephone directories in the American Midwest for those with the surname Drake. They would then contact the Mr and Mrs Drakes to let them know of their good fortune, that they would be entitled to a share of the inheritance once it had been released from the British government's coffers through legal action.

It worked – for those taking the money. Sudie Whittaker was one of those for whom the ruse worked – many times. She travelled around several US states, taking thousands of dollars from hopeful investors.

In 1914, Whittaker and her lawyer, Milo Lewis, pitched their scam at the Hartzell family farm in Iowa. Mrs Hartzell (a widow, her husband had died in 1905) was told that a "George Drake" was the rightful heir to the inheritance. He lived in Roarchport, Missouri (there isn't such a place) and was a farmer. He needed financial help to claim his inheritance, and for $25 a share, they could claim part of the eventual money. Mrs Hartzell was told that for every dollar she put in, she'd get out a hundred. Whittaker and Lewis went away with $6,500 of Mrs Hartzell's money.

When Mrs Hartzell's son, Oscar, found out he went after those who'd taken his mother's money. When he tracked them down, they told him they'd raked in $65,000 in two months. He laughed and said they were operating on too small a level. If they went big, they'd make millions. Through his mother being conned, he'd seen the possibilities of making a lot of money for himself. Oscar, who had been a deputy sheriff after leaving the family farm, faced financial problems after his own farm had failed, so joined in the scam, teaming up with Lewis and Whittaker. They formed the Sir Francis Drake Association and used it as the basis for their scheme.

He contacted people in the state of Iowa who were called Drake. Claiming to be a distant relative of the great Sir Francis, he told them that as the money was unclaimed for three centuries, it had gathered interest and was now worth $22 billion. If they wanted a share, they could join in. They would also gain a share in the city of Sir Francis's bowls-playing: Plymouth in England. Tens of thousands thought this seemed plausible and so gave him their money, all of it in some cases. The pool of targets was widened to people outside of Iowa and who didn't have Drake in their name. Those investing in the scheme became known as "Drakers".

In 1917, Hartzell crossed the Atlantic to London, supposedly to meet with Drake's heir but, in reality, to live on the proceeds of the scamming. He lived the high life, enjoying dining out and staying in a luxury apartment. He was well-dressed and enjoyed buying expensive cars. He had a mistress who gave birth to a child. Hartzell's lifestyle came at a cost, and he told investors he required more money for his considerable expenses.

When the UK government told the US Embassy in 1922 that there was no Drake estate to be claimed, Hartzell stated that it wasn't unclaimed but had belonged to a colonel called Drexel Drake. The fictional colonel had transferred the rights to the Drake estate to Hartzell when he'd become engaged to his niece. Hartzell had also acquired a title: Baron of Buckland.

The US Post Office investigated and stated that there was no unclaimed estate as Drake's wife and brother inherited it in 1597. The idea that the inheritance was still available was a myth. It made no difference – the money kept coming. Cash continued to flow into Hartzell's bank account, even during the Great Depression when money was much tighter. In 1931, he took an average of $12,000 a month. None of the Drakers seemed to wonder why, after hundreds of years, there would only be one individual who was the inheritor. Family trees tend to produce many descendants, especially after such a long period of time.

Despite this, time was running out, and the authorities in Britain and the US questioned Hartzell's associates. After 13 years of living it up on others' money, Hartzell was deported in 1933 and arrested on his arrival back in the US.

He was put on trial for mail fraud, and his supporters sent almost $130,000 to help fund his defence. The investors in the scheme had believed Hartzell when he told them the British government was doing all it could to stop the Drake estate from being released. Hartzell cited an illness suffered by the British monarch, King George V, as being due to the worry over the British economy losing all the hundreds of millions from Drake's estate. Many believed him, but the jury in his trial was wiser.

Hartzell was found guilty and given a ten-year sentence with a fine of $2,000. He is thought to have swindled two million dollars from up to 80,000 investors. Many had lost their farms after paying their life savings into the scheme.

Hartzell was sent to Leavenworth penitentiary. Even though the man running the scheme had been imprisoned for fraud, the money kept coming in: $500,000 in the year following the trial. Hartzell's associates were put on trial for this, but Hartzell himself avoided further prosecution.

SWINDLERS

He had suffered a mental collapse, fearing being the subject of an international conspiracy. Judged mentally incompetent, Hartzell was sent to a federal medical centre in 1936, where he died in 1943. What happened to his inheritance is not known.

WASHED UP

While the fabled Nigerian Princes can be difficult to track down, police were able to find one Nigerian fraudster who was not too secretive with his ill-gotten gains.

Ramon Olorunwa Abbas, aka "Ray Hushpuppi", aka "Hush", aka "Billionaire Gucci Master", was born in Nigeria in 1982. His father was a taxi driver, and his mother a marketplace bread seller in the Oworonshoki district of Lagos, Nigeria. The young Abbas made money from buying up designer clothes on sale at low prices and then selling them at a higher price to his neighbours. After operating from the boot of his car, he opened several shops, but there were suspicions that he was a "Yahoo Boy" – someone who earned money from cybercrime, in particular, romance scams.

He moved to Kuala Lumpur in 2014 and then to Dubai in the United Arab Emirates in 2017, where he stayed in the £1,000-a-night Palazzo Versace Dubai hotel.

Abbas used his Instagram handle @Hushpuppi to exhibit himself and his wealth. He was photographed in private jets or next to luxury cars like Rolls-Royces, Bentleys and Ferraris, wearing designer clothes and expensive watches – one of which, made by Richard Mille, was worth $230,000. In one image, he stands in front of a Rolls-Royce and a Bentley, wearing a Versace dressing gown with the personalized name "Hushpuppi" in gold on the back.

While in Dubai, he rubbed shoulders with English Premier League footballers, rap stars and other celebrities who visited the desert city-state. His exhibitions of his wealth earned him a large global audience: 2.3 million followers on social media.

Where did he get his money?

When interviewed on Nigerian radio, Abbas said he'd invested in real estate and had run some businesses. The interviewer accepted this as possible but did think it a bit "suspicious". This suspicion proved to be correct when, in 2020, Abbas and 11 others were raided simultaneously by police. The FBI had been alerted to possible criminal activity through Nigerian media speculation and Abbas's own Instagram, where he openly flaunted his wealth.

The police recovered $40 million in cash, 13 luxury cars (worth $6.8 million) and the names of two million potential victims. Abbas was extradited to the US. The following year, he pleaded guilty to charges including conspiracy to commit wire fraud, conspiracy to engage in money laundering and aggravated identity theft. He was ordered to pay $1.7 million in restitution.

With others, he was involved in attempting or succeeding in laundering stolen money from a cyberattack on a bank in Malta worth $14.7 million, an English Premier League football club worth $100 million and a company based in Edinburgh for $200 million.

He used the identity theft mode of operations to con almost a million dollars from a Qatari businessman on the pretext of building a school. Abbas pretended to be a bank official. On another occasion, Abbas worked with a co-conspirator to defraud a New York law firm of almost a million dollars. Abbas was able to launder money by setting up bank accounts in countries that were not too enquiring of where the deposited money came from: Bulgaria, Dubai, Mexico and Romania, among others.

As well as funding his luxurious lifestyle, Abbas used some of the money to acquire a passport for St Kitts and Nevis via a sham marriage to a St Kitts woman.

Described by the assistant director of the FBI in Los Angeles as "one of the most prolific money launderers in the world", Abbas had been involved in a form of phishing attack known as a "Business Email Compromise" (BEC). It is thought half of all BECs are sent from Nigeria, continuing the trend set by the princes from that country. The difference with a BEC attack to a mass mail-out to thousands of potential victims is that they are sent to specific targets.

The fraudster attempts to convince senior company employees (or those overseeing a company's budget) to transfer funds. To gain funds, the fraudster is able to insert themselves into corporate email accounts, intercept invoices and then replace the banking details with their own. They use fake or "spoof" emails which have the appearance of genuine ones.

The FBI thought that Abbas and the others arrested were working for a North Korean operation of cybercrime and money laundering. Three North Korean intelligence agents were charged with the cyberheist of the Maltese bank. Abbas had set up bank accounts into which $10 million from the raid was to be deposited.

In 2019, Abbas posted an Instagram photograph of himself in front of a lime-green Mercedes-Benz jeep (while dressed in matching hoodie). He wrote, "My story is filled with broken pieces, bad decisions and some ugly truths. But it is also filled with a major comeback." In November 2022, Abbas was sentenced to 11 years in prison.

CELL PHONE CRIMINAL

Prison is generally seen as the place where people are sent to prevent them from committing further crimes. This system holds true for most of the time, but in one Florida jail, a prisoner showed that his location was no barrier to criminal activities.

In 1986, Danny Faries was in Dade County Jail, awaiting trial. While on a drinking binge in Jacksonville, Florida, he shot one of his friends in the head. When the friend died in hospital two months later, Faries was charged with first-degree murder.

Prisoners in Florida jails are provided by law with "reasonable" access to a telephone. Having plenty of time on his hands to think, Faries came up with a plan that made full use of having a line to the outside world.

Faries got dozens of accomplices across the US to find discarded credit card receipts from bins and skips. He also recruited retail sales assistants who would forward credit card numbers and their holders' addresses for which the assistants were paid $20 a time.

Faries then phoned the credit card companies pretending to be from a store and asked for the customer's address and the spending limit for that card. With this information, he could phone up a store and order anything he liked. It could be hi-fis, video camcorders, TVs, computers, Armani suits, collectable gold coins or Rolex watches. He even bought airline tickets.

Faries's accomplices would then go to the address of the cardholder and intercept the delivery, take the item to a fence – a person who knowingly buys stolen goods in order to sell them for a profit – and go away with the cash, which they'd share with the scheme's mastermind. Or at least were meant to. Some of them just took the money all for themselves, proving there is no honour among thieves.

There was philanthropy among one, though: Faries used the ill-gotten cards to donate to charities he saw on TV. He also ordered flowers and jewellery for his fellow prisoners' wedding anniversaries and their partners' birthdays.

Showing a fair degree of chutzpah, Faries had goods delivered to the jail. He and his cellmates would enjoy wearing newly acquired jewellery and high-end clothes provided by this jailhouse shopping network. His generosity didn't stop at the cell block doors – Faries made sure the prison guards received gifts on their birthdays or at Christmas.

It was his largesse (albeit with others' money) that got Faries into trouble. In September 1987, he arranged a party in a high-class Miami hotel for inmates who had all been released at the same time. The party was being paid for by a Dr Entwhistle. As the party went on, hotel staff were concerned that those enjoying themselves didn't seem to be medical doctors. When the credit limit of $2,500 was reached staff spoke to one of the partygoers. A phone call from the hotel was made. Before long, Dr Entwhistle was on the line haranguing the hotel manager for the cheek in doubting his booking. The credit limit was duly extended.

When the real Dr Entwhistle saw the party on his credit card statement, he quickly got in touch with the card company. A police detective visited the hotel and came away with the phone number that had been called on the night of the party. The detective rang it and got through to a cell in Dade County Jail.

The police tapped the phone line and were amazed at the quantity of orders being created by Faries, who worked long hours. The police investigation ran into a problem when the prison authorities – who had not been informed of the police's enquiries – raided Faries's cell and found details of 300 credit cards. Despite this loss of crucial evidence, the police interviewed Faries, who told them all about it. However, he didn't face any charges for his illegal buying spree as it was felt there was insufficient evidence.

Faries was moved to a different cell where he still had access to a telephone. He had to come up with another scheme as he'd lost all the credit card numbers, bar one, which he'd written on the bottom of his bunk.

The inventive Faries used this card to place an advert in the national American newspaper *USA Today* for a cosmetic company. Readers could order merchandise at a low price. All they had to do was leave a message with an answering service providing their name, address and… credit card number. Faries was back in business. He used his new source of money to fit out the prison's gym with new equipment.

When a telephone company noticed that a huge amount of long-distance phone calls on credit card numbers were being made from one telephone, a telephone that was inside a jail, the federal authorities were called in. Secret Service agents estimated that around $2.3 million had been taken by Faries.

As he was being investigated, Faries was denied access to the telephone except for 15 minutes a day and, even then, under supervision. Was his scamming halted?

No. A telephone was run into his cell from a nearby nursing office, and Faries rigged it up so a light would flash instead of the phone ringing and giving the game away.

What did end his schemes was the murder charge. He avoided the electric chair but was given 25 years. For the credit card fraud charges, Faries was given a five-year sentence. In 1992, Faries requested his prison sentence be replaced by the death sentence as he wanted to donate his organs. His request was denied, and Faries then said it was just to get attention.

PASS THE LOOT

The 1980s were a boom time for Christian television evangelists in the US. Local cable stations and then the advent of satellite stations gave an outlet for the preaching of the Word of God. For some practitioners, however, they did not receive the blessing of the Lord but retribution of a non-divine kind: from the federal authorities.

One high-profile televangelist couple were Jim Bakker and his wife Tammy Faye. They started their religious broadcasting career in the 1960s when they appeared on Pat Robertson's Christian Broadcast Network in a variety show that appealed to children. In 1974, they started a show called *The PTL Club*, with "PTL" standing for "Praise the Lord" and "People That Love". It aired on a station broadcasting from North Carolina.

They expanded by buying up airtime on stations across the US, and then in 1978, they created a satellite network to get their message out further. *The Jim and Tammy Show* was watched by 13 million viewers each day. With Christian morals and teaching running through it, the shows featured music, drama and interviews. The Bakkers became famous. As a measure of how well-known they were and how well-regarded by the Moral Majority, the couple were invited to Ronald Reagan's presidential inauguration.

The Bakkers had grand plans, and included in them was building a Christian version of Disneyland: a theme park and hotel complex they called Heritage USA. It took up 2,300 acres and included a 500-room hotel, a water park, a Main Street USA, a castle and chapels. After opening in 1978, it became the third most visited theme park in the US, behind Disneyland and Disney World, getting almost six million visitors a year. But it was also to help bring about Jim Bakker's downfall.

For an outlay of over a thousand dollars, followers could acquire a lifetime partnership, allowing them a three-night stay each year at the yet-to-be-built Towers Hotel. There was a finite number of partners who could holiday at the hotel in a year, but Bakker and his associates continued to sell partnerships beyond this, eventually selling 153,000, raising $158 million.

For fundraising during this time, the Bakkers hosted telethons. The millions of dollars brought in were purportedly to help sustain the PTL, but it gave the Bakkers a very nice lifestyle. Between 1983 and 1987, he took $3.8 million for a salary, bonus payments and money to fund his retirement.

Properties in South Carolina, Tennessee and Florida were acquired. Lavish trips were taken to Hawaii and New York. Private jets and limousines were hired. Rolls-Royce and Mercedes cars were bought. Diamond and gold jewellery was purchased, too. PTL also paid for cosmetic surgery, shower curtains costing over $500, an air-conditioned doghouse for his pets and an air-conditioned tree house for his children. It was even claimed Bakker used the money to buy cinnamon buns to help make a hotel room smell better.

In 1987, a scandal erupted called "Pearlygate" when Jim Bakker was accused of sexually assaulting a 21-year-old church-going secretary called Jessica Hahn in a hotel in Florida seven years earlier. She was said to have been paid $265,000 hush money, the money coming from Bakker's ministry.

When the scandal broke, Bakker resigned from PTL, saying he needed to spend time with his family. The ministry and Heritage USA were taken over by fellow TV evangelist Jerry Falwell, who castigated the Bakkers. In May 1987, Falwell held a press conference where he said that the Bakkers were not fit to be in charge of PTL, that Jim had had gay relationships and that Tammy Faye had issued a set of demands so that she and her husband stayed away from PTL. These demands included generous salaries, a lakeside house and two cars. There was no love lost between the two religious practitioners: Falwell said Jim Bakker was "probably the greatest scab and cancer on the face of Christianity in 2,000 years of church history".

With donations reduced due to the scandal and money outstanding on the costs to run the park and build the Towers Hotel, there was a $72 million debt. Falwell attempted to raise money to help alleviate this. He managed to bring in $22 million – and honour a pledge to go down the park's water slide if he did so – but it was in vain. Hurricane Hugo wreaked damage to many of the buildings, and the park closed shortly afterwards.

After the scandal, the authorities began investigating the finances of PTL and the Bakkers. This resulted in Jim facing charges of mail fraud, wire fraud and conspiracy. Tammy Faye avoided criminal prosecution as she was thought not to have sufficient awareness of the fraud taking place. The day before his indictment was published, Bakker said in a sermon, "Jesus died with the federal government putting him on the cross."

Bakker's trial was not without drama. One witness collapsed while giving testimony, and Bakker's lawyer thought Jim might perform a miracle to bring him back to life. (The witness had only fainted.) Then, the following day, Bakker had a mental breakdown, hallucinating that he could see giant insects outside the courtroom. After a short spell in a psychiatric ward in a federal prison, he was back in court.

On 5 October 1989, he was found guilty on all 24 counts, and sentenced to 45 years in jail and fined half a million dollars. He appealed the sentence, and it was reduced to eight years. He served five and was released in 1994. The presiding judge, Robert Potter said before sentencing, "Those of us who have a religion are sick of being saps for money-grubbing preachers and priests."

It wasn't just Bakker who was doing well out of his followers' money. His special assistant, David Taggart, and his brother, James Taggart, were charged with tax evasion. The Taggarts had taken $1.1 million from PTL.

Tammy Faye filed for divorce while her husband was in prison and married again a year later to the contractor who built Heritage USA, Roe Messner, who was thought to have paid off Jessica Hahn. Messner served 27 months in jail for bankruptcy fraud in 1996.

Tammy Faye died in 2007 from cancer. Jim launched a new ministry called Morningside and broadcast *The Jim Bakker Show* featuring him his and second wife, Lori. The Morningside Church is situated in the Ozark Mountains in Missouri, near the border with Arkansas. As well as the chance to see live show tapings, visitors can visit the PTL shop to buy survival equipment and enquire about home and condo sales.

In 2018, Bakker claimed that the Ozarks were the best place to survive the end of days. He said on his TV show, "You're not going to live in downtown Chicago and survive the coming day... Where are you going to go when the world's on fire?"

A ROSEMARY BY ANY OTHER NAME

Rosemary Aberdour grew up in a small village in the English county of Essex. She was the only child to her middle-class parents, her father a retired doctor and her mother a medical secretary. As a youngster, Aberdour had dreams of being wealthy, but how to achieve it in reality?

After school, she completed secretarial studies, excelling in book keeping, and found work as a secretary. In 1986, she was made deputy director of the National Hospital Development Foundation. It was a charity aiming to raise £10 million for the National Hospital for Neurology and Neurosurgery.

On a salary of £20,000, Aberdour was in charge of the funds being raised, with one of her responsibilities being depositing all the donation cheques. She started stealing with £500 that paid for a holiday, as she felt she deserved a break after working 12-hour days. With her book keeping skills she was able to take a lot more without it being noticed. Cheques of amounts as big as £100,000 could be put her way.

Aberdour became chair of the committee for the Queen's Square Ball Fund, which was used to put on events for the charity. She was free to deposit money taken from the hospital fund into the Ball's account.

Going further, Aberdour started forging the signature of Richard Stevens, the charity's director. This opened up another route of acquiring money and goods. She went on to forge the signature of another, John Young, the chairman of the charity.

While money might not buy happiness, it does buy a better level of comfort. Aberdour rented a four-bedroomed penthouse apartment overlooking the River Thames in London. For the rent of £110,000 a year, it came complete with its own swimming pool, and she was looked after by a butler and her meals cooked by a personal chef.

Aberdour also spent the money on enjoying herself: a £143,000 Bentley with its purchase explained as being a raffle prize at the ball. She used the car – chauffeur-driven, of course – for her commute to work. The spend on jewellery alone was over £170,000. Champagne cost £70,000. The money was not squandered just on herself: Aberdour's pet dog Jeeves was also treated to fillet steak, delivered by the chauffeur-driven car direct from Harrods. One time, when he needed fresh air away from the Big Smoke, the pampered pooch was driven to Scotland for his "walkies".

Aberdour lived a good nightlife, too, hosting lavish parties – one of which was on a Caribbean theme, complete with tons of sand, grass-skirt-wearing guests and lobster fishing. This cost £40,000. Her Disney-themed 29th birthday party cost £63,000. Boldly going where no scammer had gone before, Aberdour spent £150,000 on a *Star Trek*-themed party with a replica *USS Enterprise* bridge in her dining room.

She organized a fortnight-long series of parties held at Thornton Watlass Hall, a Georgian-era country house in North

Yorkshire. No expense was spared, with guests enjoying lavish meals, fireworks, live entertainment, vintage car rides to horse racing events and, of course, a plentiful supply of champagne.

Aberdour treated her secretary to a medieval-themed birthday party, in a castle in Wales. Despite not being a period-authentic mode of transport, they arrived by helicopter. Jeeves – unable to be flown – was brought by car to join the fun. This party cost £40,000.

In total, Aberdour spent three-quarters of a million pounds on social events, although some who attended thought she didn't enjoy them as much as other partygoers and seemed often to be lonely. It was thought she might be organizing these events to gain affection.

Aberdour explained her apparent wealth by stating she was Lady Aberdour, an heiress to a £20 million inheritance from a Scottish earl. There was a real aristocratic family with the name Aberdour in Scotland, who were intrigued to see a supposed member of the family appear in London but took no official action.

The spending continued. She bought a personalized registration plate for her Mercedes and the Bentley. Further splurges of the charity's cash went on hiring a yacht in the Caribbean for £48,000, £55,000 on flowers and £35,000 on champagne. At her highest level of spending, she was getting through £15,000 a day.

The trust fund aristocrat was not solely focused on herself and gave money to help others, once donating £100,000 to the hospital fund. The money came from the very charity to which it was now being donated.

When the auditors came to look at the books, she skilfully managed to cover up her transgressions by transferring money, making false entries and forging documents. But by April 1991, the money from the charity had run out. The end of the road was in sight for "Lady" Aberdour.

Richard Stevens found a photocopied letter in her office featuring both his and John Young's signatures. It was addressed to a building society and asked for £250,000. When confronted by Stevens, Aberdour tried to blame it on cash flow problems and said it would be all sorted soon. She then left the country, flying to Brazil, but returned a week later.

Aberdour turned herself in to the police and subsequently pleaded guilty to charges of obtaining property by deception and theft. She had taken £2.7 million from a charity designed to help others rather than for people helping themselves to its money. Instead of a life of champagne and caviar, she faced porridge, being given four years in jail, of which she served two years, being released in October 1993.

The charities did not come out of the scandal too well, as outsiders couldn't understand how Aberdour got away with taking so much money from them. Richard Stevens moved on to another fundraising job.

Aberdour's activities provided some eventual good, as legislation was brought in to prevent such future abuses of charity money.

In 2020, Aberdour was taken to court by her brother over a hundred thousand pounds missing from their father's estate.

LA GRANDE SCAMEUR

Aberdour may have taken inspiration from a woman who operated a similar scheme a century before across the English Channel.

Thérèse Daurignac was born in the south west French countryside. Her father was a peasant farmer who liked to tell anyone within earshot that he was from an aristocratic family and there was family wealth that would be passed on to his children. Thérèse, being the oldest child, looked forward to receiving this inheritance.

When her father died, she found out quickly that there was no such inheritance. The papers describing his lucrative estate were kept in a safe, but when it was opened, they found only a house brick.

With no inheritance, Thérèse needed income and moved to Toulouse, where she found work as a laundry maid for the mayor of the city, Gustave Humbert. There, she met his son, Frederic. Thérèse told Frederic that she was due to inherit the estate of a Mademoiselle de Marcotte when she reached the age of twenty-one. Frederic, his head turned with the future promise of a chateau and vineyard, fell in love and without his father's approval, they eloped, got married, and moved to Paris.

Frederic's income as a lawyer was not enough to cover the expenses of the couple, who were enjoying the social life in the French capital. They had to ask for money from Frederic's father to pay off their creditors. The former mayor was by now a minister in the French government and couldn't afford the possibility of a scandal.

They also borrowed money, but when their creditors investigated the inheritance story, it was found to be invented – there was no Mademoiselle de Marcotte.

When faced with this damaging fact, Thérèse came up with another story. In 1879, she helped an American millionaire called Robert Henry Crawford, who was having a heart attack on a train. (She'd crawled along the outside of the train to get to his aid.) To show his gratitude, Crawford made her the sole beneficiary of his will. When he died, the money would all be hers.

But there were complications. Another, competing, will shared his estate between Thérèse's younger sister Marie and Crawford's two nephews. The nephews had signed a document allowing their uncle's lifesaver to look after the fortune while the dispute was resolved. Then, another document stated that the nephews would abandon any claim on the estate in exchange for six million francs and the opportunity for one of them to marry Marie when she reached the age of 21.

These documents were kept by Thérèse in a locked safe in her grand apartment. With this "Crawford Inheritance" as collateral, Thérèse was able to secure loans worth 65 million francs from several French banks to fund her lifestyle to which she had always thought she was entitled. The Humberts had become key figures in the social life of the wealthy and important Parisians.

Thérèse and Frederic lived in an expensive apartment they'd bought in the centre of the city, on the Avenue de la Grande Armée. They bought mansions in the countryside, but property was not the end of their spending. They also bought a steam-powered yacht. Family was not forgotten, and Thérèse included her sister and brothers in the spending sprees in Parisian boutiques and restaurants.

However, there was potential trouble when a banker from Lyon, who was in the French capital to discuss another loan, enquired as to where this Robert Crawford had lived. Thérèse told him Boston. When the banker subsequently visited Boston and asked about Crawford, he discovered there was no such person. The banker informed a contact in France, but he was unable to tell anyone else as his body was soon afterwards found in a river in New York. Whether he jumped or was pushed was a source of conjecture, with the latter being favoured. When Thérèse was asked about the non-existent American millionaire, she just brushed it off.

While enjoying their lavish lifestyle, Thérèse and Frederic and her siblings faced a large obstacle to their scheme: Marie was approaching the age when the safe had to be opened and the inheritance released.

Thérèse came up with two strategies. She conceived of a fake legal challenge over the inheritance of Robert Crawford's two nephews, with her brothers playing the part of the nephews. Her second ploy was to set up an insurance business called Rente Viagere. It proved popular, and investors poured money in: 40 million francs. They were well-rewarded – or at least the original investors were, as it was a form of a Ponzi scheme. Thérèse's brothers used some of the money to pay off creditors who were insistent on being paid.

This scheme was to bring them all down. A banker found there were no investments being made by this finance company. Allegations were published in a French newspaper. It led to demands that the legendary safe be opened. When it was, its contents were revealed to be... a house brick.

Thousands of investors were left high and dry. Some of those who were wiped out financially took their own lives.

Thérèse and family had fled but were eventually arrested in Madrid in 1902. When the police were looking for them, they raided the renowned artist Henri Matisse's studio. His mother-in-law was Thérèse's housekeeper and seen as involved in the fraud.

Thérèse and Frederic were given five years of hard labour, with her brothers getting shorter jail terms. Marie escaped any charges, being seen as a bystander while the swindle was taking place.

It was thought that, after being released, Thérèse may have ended her days in the US.

MR NATWARLAL

In India, a con artist who pulls off a great scam is called a "Natwarlal" in honour of India's great artist of the swindle.

Much about his life is shrouded in mystery, but it is thought he was born Mithilesh Kumar Srivastava in 1912 in a village in the north east of India. His first venture into the criminal world was when he forged a neighbour's signature to cash cheques. When the neighbour found he was a thousand rupees in debt, Natwarlal – a name he had adopted – moved swiftly to Calcutta, where he started studying for a business degree while also working as a broker in the stock market.

Natwarlal was arrested for the first time in 1937 after claiming a large quantity of iron was his and then reselling it. He was sentenced to six months of hard labour, but this didn't put him off committing further offences.

Across over half a century of criminal activity, he used more than 50 aliases, coupled with his skills in forgery, to bring success in conning numerous places such as shops, jewellers, banks and railway stations. One time, he scammed 650,000 rupees from the Punjab National Bank via a fraud, which involved getting cash advances on forged receipts for rice bags being transported.

A typical Natwarlal operation was like the one he pulled off in August 1987. Smartly dressed, he entered a watch store in New Delhi's Connaught Place. Posing as the personal assistant to the government's minister of finance, N. D. Tiwari, he told the shop's owner that members of his boss's political party were to be given watches at an upcoming meeting. He would need 93 watches.

The next day, Natwarlal returned to the shop in a chauffeur-driven car and requested that a shop assistant accompany him to the ministry building known as the North Block. There, Natwarlal walked into the building before emerging with a bank draft for 32,829 rupees. This was exchanged for the watches, and two days afterwards, the bank draft was declared to be a forgery. The experienced grifter had managed the watch con several times in different cities. Just a few months after his success in New Delhi, he tried it again in Gorakhpur, but the owner cottoned on, and the police were called. Natwarlal was arrested once again.

He also targeted foreign visitors. Perhaps following the example of the "Bouncing Czech" Victor Lustig, Natwarlal sold several famous buildings in India. The Parliament House was sold to a non-Indian national, and it was said that Natwarlal included the members of parliament in the sale. He also sold the Taj Mahal (three times), Delhi's historic Mughal Red Fort (twice) and the presidential palace and former viceroy's residence, the Rashtrapati Bhavan (once).

Natwarlal earned the admiration of ordinary Indians and was mobbed by crowds when he was recognized. As had happened for America's great conman Frank Abagnale, so it was for India's, when a movie was made of his life. Bollywood superstar Amitabh Bachchan played *Mr Natwarlal* to great acclaim in 1979.

The real-life con artist earned further affection from average, modest Indians by passing on some of his ill-gotten gains to them. He was seen as an Indian Robin Hood – stealing from the rich and giving to the poor. One time, after returning to his home village in triumph, Natwarlal gave each villager 100 rupees after a feast he'd arranged for them.

Natwarlal's activity did not go unnoticed, and he was arrested an estimated ten times but often used his guile to escape. After being jailed in 1957 in Kanpur, Natwarlal received a police uniform in exchange for handing the jailer a box full of money. Natwarlal then walked out wearing the uniform. The guards at the outside gates saluted this departing officer. When Natwarlal's getaway car broke down, it did not faze him: he got into a hearse to continue his escape. The jailer who was bribed was disappointed to find they had let this wily prisoner go for a box filled not with cash but with newspapers. Only the top layer was bank notes.

His criminal endeavours inspired others, keen to earn money by their wits. When arrested in Uttar Pradesh in 1987 after allegations of being involved in several criminal acts, Natwarlal said, "There are hundreds of thieves who posed as me. But I'm the real Natwarlal."

He received prison sentences totalling 113 years, but it is thought he only ever spent 20 years of his life locked up. He was wanted in eight states, but his situation was helped at times by the intervention of nature. The police in Lucknow lost their files on him following a flood.

In June 1996, now an elderly wheelchair user, he was arrested for the last time. When being transferred to hospital for treatment, this frail 84-year-old gave his accompanying police officers the slip and disappeared at New Delhi railway station.

For a life that was full of trickery, it was not unexpected that there would be something similar in death. In 2009, Natwarlal's lawyer asked that the 100 outstanding charges against his client be dropped as Natwarlal had died in July of that year. However, Natwarlal's brother came forward to state that he had died 13 years before.

In 2011, plans were made to erect a statue of a famous son of the Bihar state. Not Rajendra Prasad, India's first president, born in Ziradei, but his country's most famous conman: Natwarlal in his home village of Bangra. It almost goes without saying that the master forger had once forged Prasad's signature as part of a con.

A senior policeman in Patna said in 1987, when this elusive and almost mythical figure had been caught (after escaping custody by faking an illness seven years previously), "As a conman, he is unmatched in the annals of Indian crime."

CAPTAIN BOB

Two rival figures dominated the British newspaper world in the 1980s. Sharing the same initials, they were Rupert Murdoch and Robert Maxwell. Both were foreign nationals; Murdoch was an Australian, and Maxwell came from Czechoslovakia. One died in 1991 in circumstances shrouded in mystery.

Robert Maxwell was born Ján Ludvík Hyman Binyamin Hoch in 1923. An Orthodox Jew, he was brought up in a peasant farming background in an area of Czechoslovakia that is now part of Ukraine. He was able to escape Nazi persecution (unlike several members of his family who died in Auschwitz) and, in France in 1940, joined the Czech army in exile.

As "Ivan du Maurier", he was evacuated to Britain when the Nazis occupied mainland Europe. When the Allies invaded north west Europe in 1944, Maxwell fought as part of the British Army, reaching Germany in 1945. During the fighting, he was awarded the Military Cross for bravery in attacking a German position. He was commissioned as an officer and reached the rank of captain.

After the war ended, Maxwell remained in Germany, interrogating prisoners. It was later alleged that he operated in the black market, buying and selling contraband such as cigarettes, and then acted as an agent for the KGB. It was further alleged that he presented himself as an asset to Britain's intelligence agency MI6.

After Maxwell left the army, he became a British citizen and, in 1964, stood for election to the Houses of Parliament. He became Labour MP for Buckingham until being voted out in 1970. This left him more time for his main pursuit: publishing. After the war, in 1951, he founded a company called Pergamon Press, which printed science journals. Maxwell oversaw growth in the company's output and profitability. In 1951, Maxwell acquired Britain's biggest book wholesale company, Simpkin Marshall. The company loaned money to other companies controlled by its owner, and it was liquidated in 1955, owing almost £700,000.

In 1969, Maxwell lost his place on the board of Pergamon. Takeover discussions had taken place with an American company, but Maxwell had overstated the value of the encyclopaedia-producing arm of his company. He had also used transactions between his private family companies and Pergamon to raise the share price. He didn't face criminal charges but was investigated by the British government's Department of Trade. Their report stated, "Notwithstanding Mr Maxwell's acknowledged abilities and energy, he is not in our opinion a person who can be relied upon to exercise proper stewardship of a publicly quoted company." In 1974, Maxwell bought Pergamon back but kept it as a private company.

He was keen to expand into other areas, such as newspapers, and, in 1968 he tried to buy the British tabloid *News of the World,* but his socialist leanings and foreign origins put off the owners. They then sold it to an Australian, Rupert Murdoch, who also bought *The Sun.*

Maxwell finally achieved his aim of owning a British newspaper with the acquisition of the Mirror Group in 1984. It published the popular tabloids *Daily Mirror*, *Sunday People*, the Scottish *Daily Record* and *Sunday Mail*. He later bought the New York tabloid, *Daily News*.

It was not the last takeover he pursued, and a series of bids were made throughout the 1980s. Maxwell acquired Macmillan Publishers (for $2.6 billion), Official Airline Guide (for $750 million), a UK classical record company, Berlitz language schools, and a half-share of MTV Europe. He bought English football league club Oxford United in 1982 and saw them promoted to the English top division and win the league cup. He almost bought Manchester United Football Club, but the price was too steep.

Maxwell claimed that his empire was not built on debt as his rival Murdoch's was, but this statement was not on solid ground. The share price of his company, Maxwell Communications Corporation (MCC), started to fall in 1990. Maxwell sold Pergamon (for £440 million) and 49 per cent of Mirror Group Newspapers to help reduce his debts.

A BBC documentary alleged that Maxwell had been carrying out a similar scheme as he'd done in the late 1960s, using his private companies to make transactions to boost the share price of MCC.

Worse was to come.

In November 1991, he was on his yacht, the *Lady Ghislaine*, off the Canary Islands. The boat was named after one of his children, his daughter Ghislaine. Maxwell and his wife Betty had nine children, with five of them working at his companies.

On the morning of 5 November, the ship's crew went to wake Maxwell but found his cabin empty. A search was carried out, and his naked body was found a few hours later, floating in the sea.

The mortifying demise of an intensely proud man who courted publicity and influence was a major news story. What had happened?

The inquest stated he'd died from a heart attack and accidental drowning. Speculation that had started when he went missing continued. Had he been murdered? There were rumours of possible action by Israeli intelligence unit Mossad. Was it an accident? He was known to urinate into the ocean from the stern of his yacht, so had he lost his footing and gone overboard? Was it suicide? He had missed a meeting with the Bank of England over his company's defaulting for over £50 million, but his sons thought it not part of his mentality to take his own life.

Within weeks, the truth started to emerge. Maxwell's companies were in huge debt. It was then discovered that Maxwell had stolen money: £933 million from his companies, including £448 million from the Mirror Group and MCC company pension funds to try to shore his empire up.

Maxwell's two sons, Kevin and Ian, were left to pick up the pieces, but the companies filed for bankruptcy protection in 1992. Kevin, CEO of MCC, saw his company's shares halve in value in four days' trading. Trading was later ceased in MCC and Mirror Group (Ian was chairman of the group).

The two brothers were charged with fraud but, after an eight-month trial, were acquitted. Government legislation was brought in to prevent future abuses of company pension funds.

Newsweek magazine called Maxwell the "Crook of the Century". The 32,000 former Mirror Group pensioners received half what they were due.

TROUBLE DOWN UNDER

The title of who deserves the label "world's greatest living con artist" can be debated, with strong cases for many of those already described. One candidate with a definite chance is Australian Peter Foster. He has conned figures from all walks of society and earned himself a lot of publicity while doing so.

Born in 1962, Foster hails from Australia's Gold Coast, where he started as an entrepreneur while still in his teens. A former classmate recalled how the young Foster returned from a holiday in the Philippines with a haul of fake designer watches he was looking to sell at their high school.

He moved on to promoting special nights at a disco despite being underage to actually enter the club. When aged 20, he ran into trouble with the authorities. Foster had begun promoting boxing matches, but when one bout was cancelled, he made a fraudulent insurance claim for which he was later fined.

While financial failure is a common feature of successful businessmen, it came early for Foster, who was declared bankrupt after promoting a boxing match featuring legendary pugilist Muhammad Ali that didn't transpire.

In 1986, Foster arrived in the UK to promote his weight loss drink: Bai Lin tea. The tea was denounced on British national

TV as being sold through a pyramid scheme. The product was not as advertised: it was commonplace black Chinese tea. This breach of trade description legislation resulted in a £5,000 fine. It was alleged that Foster was receiving £5,000 from each of the hundred distributors. The company behind the tea, Slimweight, went into voluntary liquidation with debts of three-quarters of a million pounds.

While in the UK, he started a relationship with tabloid newspaper pin-up model Samantha Fox. She was the marketing face of his business venture. When Fox found out she was not the only woman he was wooing, they split. Another well-known person to endorse the tea was Sarah Ferguson, the then-wife of Prince Andrew.

Foster was not deterred and, in 1988, came up with another slimming scheme. He recruited Michelle Deakin, the 19-year-old winner of a young slimmer of the year competition, to say she had used his "Deakin Diet" to win, but the granules being sold were nothing but the thickening agent guar gum.

Foster fled to Australia before facing charges. He did not abandon the tea-making venture, taking it to the US and selling it as Chow Lo tea in 1989. It was said to lower cholesterol, but as this was not true, charges were brought. Foster was found guilty of conspiracy to commit grand theft; he served four months in a Los Angeles jail before returning to Australia.

Once back Down Under, he sold franchises to a "contour treatment" said to reduce the size of women's thighs. Foster was charged with making false claims and fined AUD $15,000.

On his return to Britain in 1994, Foster's past caught up with him, and he was fined £25,000 over the Bai Lin tea venture. Then in 1996, he was given a two-year jail sentence for falsely advertising the non-slimming granules. While on day release from an open prison, Foster fled to Australia using a false passport.

In 1998, British authorities wanted Foster extradited, but he resisted for 18 months, claiming he was in danger as he'd acted as an informant on prison officers. In 2000, the extradition finally took place, and when back in Britain, Foster was given a jail sentence of 33 months after fraudulently gaining credit for a company called Foremost Body Corporation, which was selling thigh-reduction products.

With time served in Australia being counted, he was released. Foster was banned from being a company director, and he returned to Australia.

In 2001, Foster moved to Fiji and became involved in politics, working for a candidate in the country's general election. The next year, he was back in the UK, acting as the managing director of a company called Renuelle, which made TRIMit slimming pills. This was inside a five-year ban for acting as a company director, and he was investigated by British authorities.

Foster got involved with the highest levels of politics when "Cheriegate" came to light later that year. Cherie Blair was the wife of Tony Blair, at that time the UK's prime minister. She had bought two flats in Bristol with the assistance of her friend Carole Caplin's boyfriend, Peter Foster. This was said to be in return for her helping him with a current extradition procedure by the Australian authorities. When it came to light, Cherie Blair tried to distance herself from Foster, but the scandal damaged the Blairs' reputation.

Foster distanced himself from Britain by moving to Ireland, but in January of the following year, 2003, he was deported to

Australia. Back in Australia, there was an investigation into another slimming venture: the TRIMit pills and the company behind promoting them. Foster's involvement in Chaste Corporation had been kept quiet as it took AUD $1 million from those paying AUD $40,000 each to get the rights to sell the pills. In 2005, Foster and Chaste Corporation were fined for price fixing and misleading conduct.

That year, Foster returned to Fiji. He had gained entry to the country through forged documents, attempting to hide his criminal past and gain a work visa. The irrepressible con artist tried to escape custody by stripping to his underwear and jumping into a river, where he hit his head on a boat's propellers, although he later claimed his injuries were the result of harsh treatment by the police.

After a hunger strike in hospital over the alleged police beatings, Foster faced charges in court for the forged documents that assisted his entry to the country, plus other charges over a beach resort development. It was alleged Foster had attempted to disparage a rival's plans for the resort in order for him and his Fijian associates to gain control of the venture.

In January 2007, while awaiting trial, Foster skipped bail and left Fiji for Vanuatu, travelling by boat and wading ashore. Vanuatu's police arrested him for illegal entry, and despite an attempt to fake illness, he made a court appearance, after which he spent three weeks in jail. Showing his charm and powers of persuasion, Foster persuaded the authorities to allow him to spend the last weekend of his sentence in a luxury hotel. He was then once more deported to Australia. At the time, Foster said, "I go from one catastrophe to another. I don't know how I do it. I'm going to have to learn eventually, I suppose."

Would he?

Once back home, there was no let-up. Foster immediately faced charges of fraud and money laundering over forged documents he had used to gain a $300,000 loan from a bank in Micronesia. He had claimed the money was for a tourist development, but it had been used to pay rent on his partner's home and credit card debt. Foster served 18 months of a 54-month sentence for this.

In 2011 and 2012, Foster was back in court in Australia over advertising a weight loss nasal spray called SensaSlim. During the trial, it came to light that he referred to himself as the "International Man of Mischief". Foster was charged with contempt of court for working in the weight-loss industry when he had been banned in 2005. In 2016, Foster was fined the maximum amount of AUD $660,000 and banned from being a company director for scamming 90 investors for AUD $6 million. SensaSlim was also fined – they'd kept Foster's involvement hidden from investors. The judge at Foster's trial said he was "beyond redemption". He received a three-year prison sentence for contempt of court, but Foster failed to appear in court, so was sentenced in absentia.

Foster suggested he was in Fiji, but the police tracked him down in New South Wales. In trying to resist arrest, his pants fell which didn't help the attempt, and he was sent to jail for his outstanding contempt of court conviction.

Foster had been busy while on the run, going under an assumed name "Mark Hughes" – and running an online sports betting operation called the Sports Trading Club, which was said to have been a Ponzi scheme taking AUD $10 million from victims. In 2015, Foster was released from prison, allegedly due to acting as an informant to the prison authorities.

In 2020, Foster was once again arrested, while walking his dogs on a beach in north Queensland, after being linked to a sports betting firm called Sport Predictions, which was alleged to be a ruse for Foster – or "William Dawson" as he was now known – to scam money with no bets being made. He was alleged to have duped a Hong Kong businessman out of $1.9 million in Bitcoins.

When he failed to turn up at court in May 2021, an arrest warrant was issued, and he was arrested in December that year. The case continued into 2022. Foster was granted bail but had to wear an ankle tag, surrender his passport and not travel more than 50 km from his home. He said, "People will be going to jail over this, but it won't be me."

THE CON OF AFRICA

The "long con" is, as its name suggests, one that is performed over an extended period of time. The con artist is prepared to drag it out in order to maximize the takings, but this requires sufficient time to have sustained credibility and for their victims to keep believing that it will turn out okay in the end.

One of the most remarkable long cons was perpetuated by a Ghanaian man called John Ackah Blay-Miezah, born in 1941 in a village in what was known then as the Gold Coast. It had been part of the British Empire since the middle of the nineteenth century.

The young Ghanaian received a scholarship and went to study in the US at the University of Pennsylvania in 1959. He enjoyed the student life but didn't actually enrol. Instead of studying, he worked in an exclusive club in Philadelphia as a busboy.

When he returned to Ghana in 1963, he said he had to meet the president of the country. Fearing a threat to Kwame Nkrumah, who had led his country to independence in 1957, Blay-Miezah was imprisoned.

Kwame Nkrumah faced a difficult period as the country's economy faltered in the 1960s. It had also lost money through bad investments by the UK government. With government reserves being used up as debts rose, rumours started that Nkrumah had siphoned millions of dollars of the country's money abroad.

Blay-Miezah was one of the prisoners released after a coup that deposed Nkrumah in 1966. While inside, Blay-Miezah had spent time learning how to act, walk and talk as a "big man" from the older, powerful men he shared the jail with.

He put his acquired skills to use in 1971 when operating as a banker in West Africa. He would take fees for setting up loans to businesses – and then disappear. Once he had amassed a few hundred Ghanaian cedi, he'd quickly leave the area to set up in another town to do the same, in classic con artist style.

One day, Blay-Miezah bumped into his former teacher, Kofi Bentum Quantson. Quantson now worked for Ghana's Special Branch police department. His former pupil told him he had been falsely imprisoned while in the US and received millions of dollars in compensation, but he had since had difficulty getting the money into Ghana.

Quantson was puzzled as getting money into the country wasn't normally a problem. When he enquired at police HQ, he discovered Blay-Miezah was wanted after jumping bail for a petty fraud case. Blay-Miezah was arrested but managed to escape by faking a heart attack. On the way to hospital, he asked to withdraw money from a bank to pay his medical bill. He went to the toilet in the bank and disappeared through a trap door in the pit latrine.

It wasn't to be the last time he escaped when things looked about to end.

Blay-Miezah next appeared in Liberia as a doctor. He told the hotel he was staying at that the bill would be paid by the

Ghanaian embassy. When Ghana's ambassador denied any such agreement, Blay-Miezah disappeared.

His travels next took him to the US, to Philadelphia. At his hotel, Blay-Miezah said he was a diplomat from Ghana's Washington embassy, and they would settle the bill. When the $2,700 bill was presented to the embassy, staff there were surprised. They had no diplomat staying at this hotel. Blay-Miezah didn't escape this time and was given a sentence of 1–2 years in jail for fraud. The prison psychiatrist said of him, "I feel this man cannot distinguish reality from fantasy."

Blay-Miezah faced deportation, so he married an American woman after telling her he was a 49-year-old doctor and the son of a tribal chief. Green card secured; they were divorced months later.

The charming con artist then started telling a story that was to be the basis of his long con. It went like this: Nkrumah had exported vast amounts of Ghana's gold and cash to Switzerland. The money was to be used for the Ghanaian people and was moved so it would not be stolen or misused. It was held in a trust fund: the Oman Ghana Trust Fund (OGTF) entrusted on Nkrumah's deathbed to one man, Dr John Ackah Blay-Miezah.

The money would restore Ghana after ruinous colonialism. Electricity, homes, education, infrastructure – they would all be paid for with this money. To release these funds, Blay-Miezah needed money. Investors would get a 10:1 return on each dollar. Tens of millions of dollars – possibly as much as a hundred million – were paid over.

Not everyone was hoodwinked. The Ghanaian authorities, well aware of Blay-Miezah's past, warned that he was a wanted man. The US secretary of state, Henry Kissinger, alerted every US embassy and consulate that it was a fraudulent operation. The US ambassador to Ghana, the former child movie star Shirley Temple Black, always had doubts about the legitimacy of a story that attracted so much good faith – and money.

Blay-Miezah was able to convince Ghana's new head of state Colonel Acheampong that he would return the fund's money to Ghana. (Acheampong had taken control of the country in 1972, the sixth leader since Nkrumah had been deposed in 1966). Blay-Miezah argued he needed a diplomatic passport to pursue the money. He was released from the prison where he had been held on fraud charges and left Ghana.

Whether in Ghana, the US or London, he lived well, being driven by a chauffeur and staying in the finest of hotels, with his own chef on hand to cook him Ghanaian meals. Blay-Miezah continued trying to convince banks and investors that the fund was real, that funds would be released, and that everyone would get their money.

If he faced a setback, he just tried again. In 1975, after an attempt failed to get $10 million paid into a Ghanaian bank in London, he went on to persuade a Swiss bank that he was the fund's trustee and received a letter stating this "fact". With this "proof", he could convince investors to keep on paying in. And pay in they did. One US lawyer invested a million dollars.

One way to ensure that he couldn't face future charges was to reach high office, and Blay-Miezah stood for election as Ghana's president. To the horror of those not taken in by his story, it looked like Ghana's first multi-millionaire might win. His plans were scuppered by being put on trial for bribery, forgery and perjury.

During the trial, it was revealed he had fooled the university in Pennsylvania and claimed his roommate's degrees in his name. Blay-Miezah was found guilty and sent to prison for nine years. He only spent a year inside, being released after a successful appeal: he said he needed medical attention for a range of ailments and went to London where instead of going to hospital, he started living in a penthouse suite in a luxury hotel.

The money was still coming into the fund from Asia as well as Europe and the US, although some investors were getting anxious about the delays in getting a return on their investment. Despite his repeated promises, the cigar-smoking charmer never managed to pay them back. There was always some reason, be it a technical issue with the banks or those in the Ghanaian government who didn't like how popular he was and were obstructing the money being released.

As the months and years went by into the 1980s, investors lost patience. One American investor who'd put in all his money went to Ghana and drove a car at Blay-Miezah's house gates to try to get to him. In 1983, former US attorney John Mitchell, jailed for his part in the Watergate scandal, began working for Blay-Miezah to give his project some legitimacy in return for his share of the future money.

In 1985, Blay-Miezah was ordered back to Ghana as the junta in charge was worried he was only working for himself. He was arrested then released, talking his way out of trouble one more time, saying if he didn't sort it out, the junta could shoot him.

In 1986, an associate in the US, Robert Ellis, who was in charge of soliciting money in the US, faced 30 felony charges, including theft. The prosecuting district attorney said, "It was the biggest fraud in the history of Philadelphia."

Still, Blay-Miezah continued with his scheme. In Austria, investors flew out to receive their payout. Months went by. They received nothing. Then, the ringmaster told them that banks in Guernsey would release the money. They flew there. Another delay. Investors were told that the banks were holding up the release of money as they'd lent it out to others.

In 1988, he led them to the Cayman Islands. Again, there was no payout, and Blay-Miezah fled. Back in London and under pressure from investors, he experienced a heart attack and went to a private Harley Street doctor rather than accident and emergency at a public NHS hospital.

In 1988, Blay-Miezah was interviewed for American TV show *60 Minutes*. He said, "I have been branded as a confidence man. I say I have not defrauded anyone." During the show, it was stated that Nkrumah couldn't have given the fund to Blay-Miezah on his deathbed because when he died, Blay-Miezah was in prison in the US. Blay-Miezah was forced by the Ghanaian government to admit that Nkrumah had nothing to do with the Oman Ghana Trust Fund.

After several decades, Blay-Miezah's scheme had reached the end of the road. He returned to Ghana, where he was placed under house arrest. The great long con artist tried to get out of the country one more time, but his powers of persuasion failed.

After three years of house arrest, rumours spread in the summer of 1992 that the man who had promised so much had died. A few months later, in the US, a grand jury indicted him on five counts of wire fraud. When the US authorities were told the accused had died, they insisted on having fingerprints taken from his corpse. With Blay-Miezah, even in death, no one was quite sure what was true and what was not.

The plausibility of the background story still had the power to convince years later. In 2008, another Ghanaian announced himself to be the sole trustee of the Oman Ghana Trust Fund. Only he had the password to unlock the riches – all $3.2 trillion of it.

FINAL WORD

It is clear that the human desire to make – or take – money that isn't theirs shows no signs of diminishing. The centuries of crafty and ingenious con artists taking victims' money look set to continue. While snake oil from the nineteenth century might not be sold as much today, other supposed health cures and fake medicines can be purchased online – and you never know, it might never turn up after your money has been banked.

Technology will be used in new and inventive ways. In 2023, British money expert Martin Lewis was alerted to a deep fake scam. The scammers used AI technology to replicate his face and voice for a video extolling an investment app supposedly backed by Elon Musk. Lewis, who never does advertisements, tweeted, "This is frightening. Government and regulators must step up to stop big tech publishing such dangerous fakes. People'll lose money and it'll ruin lives." Other celebrities who have been used to falsely endorse investment scams include businessman Sir Richard Branson, musician Ed Sheeran and action movie actor Jason Statham.

While the method and manner might be different, scammers and swindlers are still on the lookout for a way to persuade you – the person with what they want: money – to hand it over.

And by the time you notice you've been duped, the con artist and your cash are far away.

CULTS: COERCION AND CONTROL

The World's Most Notorious Cults
(And The People Who Escaped Them)

Jamie King

ISBN: 978-1-83799-280-5

Belief system or brainwashing? Captivated or captive? Community or cult? Uncover stories of the world's most infamous cults in this true crime compendium... Filled with stories of notorious cults, this book details their origins, beliefs, leaders, followers and victims, and uncovers the unthinkable horrors hidden by these "utopian" societies.